YOUR
ECO-FRIENDLY
H⌂ME

Buying, Building, or Remodeling Green

Sid Davis

⸸AMACOM

American Management Association

New York • Atlanta • Brussels • Chicago • Mexico City • San Francisco
Shanghai • Tokyo • Toronto • Washington, D. C.

Special discounts on bulk quantities of AMACOM books are
available to corporations, professional associations, and other
organizations. For details, contact Special Sales Department,
AMACOM, a division of American Management Association,
1601 Broadway,
New York, NY 10019.
Tel: 212-903-8316. Fax: 212-903-8083.
E-mail: specialsls@amanet.org
Website: www. amacombooks.org/go/specialsales
To view all AMACOM titles go to: www.amacombooks.org

This publication is designed to provide accurate and authoritative
information in regard to the subject matter covered. It is sold with
the understanding that the publisher is not engaged in rendering
legal, accounting, or other professional service. If legal advice or other
expert assistance is required, the services of a competent professional
person should be sought.

*REALTOR® is a registered collective membership mark that identifies a real estate
professional who is a member of the NATIONAL ASSOCIATION OF REALTORS® and
subscribes to its strict code of ethics.*

Library of Congress Cataloging-in-Publication Data

Davis, Sid, 1944-
  Your eco-friendly home : buying, building, or remodeling green / Sid Davis.
      p. cm.
  Includes index.
  ISBN-13:978-0-8144-1037-0
  ISBN-10:0-8144-1037-5
  1. Residential real estate—United States. 2. House buying—United States.
  3. Ecological houses—United States. 3. Residential real estate—Environmental aspects.
  5. Sustainable living. I. Title.

  HD259.D396 2009
  643'.12—dc22

                                                                        2008026401

Printing number

10 9 8 7 6 5 4 3 2 1

CONTENTS

INTRODUCTION

Over the past few decades, the awareness that resources are finite and that the materials we use and our methods of disposal are harming our environment is reaching critical mass. So many people are now demanding that these problems be addressed that builders, suppliers, homebuyers, and remodelers are listening,

As a result, working with natural materials, energy conservation, and recycling are becoming mainstream, and even mandatory in some areas. And homebuyers are starting to demand green building products, appliances, and recycled materials.

Actually, recycling began long ago on the American frontier. When early settlers needed to move, it is said they would burn down their cabins to reclaim the nails, which could be used in building their next home.

While we no longer burn down our homes to reclaim materials, more homeowners than ever are becoming recycling conscious. They are separating their trash and taking old appliances, fixtures, and construction debris to recycling centers. And from these recycled materials, companies are emerging that are able to turn them into stunning countertops, insulation, cabinets, flooring, roofing, and just about every building product you would need to build your green home.

To further advance the green movement, governments and building trade associations are realizing that this is not just a passing fad; it's serious and it's the future. The growing consensus today among builders and suppliers is, either get with the programs or risk being left behind.

And like a sluggish giant, this country's homeowners are starting to stir and realize that eco-friendly and energy efficient buildings are the best ways to go. With a little prodding and more education, homeowners are certain to demand and buy homes constructed to green home building standards.

To further help the green building movement, the National Association of Home Builders (NAHB), whose members build about 80 percent of the country's new homes each year, has adopted a green building standard for its members.

Another giant in the green building industry, the U.S. Green Building Council (USGBC), has launched its version of the LEED® (Leadership in Energy & Environmental Design) certification program. The LEED rating system for green homes has four award levels—certified, silver, gold, and platinum. Your rating depends on the number of points you score for sustainability, energy efficiency, environmental impact, design, and so on.

These standards put green builders, manufacturers, and suppliers on the same page, speaking the same language. What all this means to you as a homeowner or prospective owner is that you can be assured that when you buy, build, or remodel a home to these standards, you're getting what you want and what you're paying for.

From the homeowners' perspective, as the competition for energy, land, building resources, and a reasonable commute becomes more challenging, it's obvious that changes are needed to maintain the lifestyle the majority of us want. And that means we are going to have to incorporate resource management and recycling into our lives and evangelize others to do the same in order to make a noticeable difference.

Of course, this not only applies to conservation but to taking on the personal responsibility of educating ourselves and seeking out products and processes that are energy and environmentally positive.

Builders build, manufacturers make, and suppliers stock what homeowners buy. If we demand green products, more and better building and energy efficient products will appear on the market.

One successful example is the Department of Energy's Energy Star® program (www.energystar.gov), which rates appliances for their energy efficiency. This program has made it easier for us to determine up-front if a home or its components are energy efficient and meet specific environmental standards. The program is so successful that the rating expanded to cover insulation, fixtures, windows and other building products. And it happened because we consumers voted for it with our checkbooks and credit cards.

As you're probably aware, the current popular buzz word for environmental awareness and energy efficiency is "green." And why not? Green is a good nature color even though not everyone looks good wearing it, according to my wife.

Throughout the book, I'll use the terms "green" and "eco-friendly" interchangeably to refer to environmentally friendly, and energy efficient organizations, products, and ideas. The intent here is to clarify and ease communication, not to advance any political agenda or belief.

Interestingly, over the past twenty-five years I've noticed that many homeowners want to be more environmentally responsible by saving energy and using sustainable products. First time homeowners especially have wanted to become more involved but haven't known how to start. It's for these homebuyers especially that this book has been written.

The route I've suggested for beginning homebuyers is to buy a home and then fix it up to be energy efficient. Although few can afford to remodel green all at once, they can do projects as their budget allows, and eventually they'll have a green home they can be proud to live in. Many homebuyers start out with this intent but get discouraged because they don't have a plan of action.

For those who are already home owners and want to make their homesite eco-friendly, I've suggested ways to help them triage their projects so that they can attain their goal of a green home. While it may take a while, the result will be worth it.

Included as well is a chapter of tips and traps to avoid for first-time homeowners who want to buy or build a new home from a green builder. Many builders advertise their projects as green, but in reality they overlook many energy-saving possibilities.

For those who have a building lot and are excited about building their eco-friendly dream home, I've also included tips on finding a green architect who shares your dream and working with a builder to make it a reality.

Throughout this book I've tried, without getting too technical, to provide an overview of the products both needed and available to create an eco-friendly home. If you want more data on specific items, check out the websites offered in the sidebars.

This book is divided into three parts. The first part focuses on finding, financing, and buying an eco-friendly home. This includes qualifying for an Energy Efficient Mortgage (EEM); finding an eco-friendly agent to work with you to find green properties, as well as shopping for an green home on your own. There are also successful strategies you can use when making an offer on a home, getting sellers to pay concessions, and buying a home warranty to save yourself money.

The second part deals with building an eco-friendly home. This includes finding and working with a green architect; planning your new green home, which is comprised of using passive energy saving options, ventilating your new home, determining whether solar or wind power are for you, and using sustainable products and cutting costs; and green landscaping, which focuses on creating a landscaping plan of action, working with the characteristics of your soil, determining where and what to plant, planning a sustainable landscape, and applying and conserving water.

The third part of the book covers remodeling to make your existing home eco-friendly. This includes chapters on planning your green remodel and working with a green architect and contractors; remodeling your home's exterior with eco-friendly materials, with a special emphasis on making your roof environmentally friendly, replacing your siding with eco-friendly materials, upgrading to energy efficient windows, using eco-friendly stains and paints, building an environmentally friendly deck, patio, or fence, and recycling and disposing of construction waste; and remodeling your home's interior with eco-friendly systems and materials, focusing on ventilating your energy efficient home, upgrading your heating and cooling systems to make them energy efficient, choosing and using eco-friendly stains and paints, selecting eco-friendly floor coverings, remodeling your kitchen using green appliances and materials, and upgrading your bathroom with eco-friendly fixtures and materials.

While no book can detail everything that's happening with the rapidly expanding green real estate movement, *Your Eco-Friendly Home* will give you an overview and a good starting point. Whether you're planning to buy, build, or remodel to have a home that's environmentally friendly, be assured that your efforts and contribution to protecting our resources and reducing our energy dependence is important to us all.

PART 1

FINDING, FINANCING, AND BUYING AN ECO-FRIENDLY HOME

CHAPTER 1

FINDING AND QUALIFYING FOR ECO-FRIENDLY FINANCING

Whether you're buying your first or twentieth home, the first step should be to find a mortgage lender and get pre-approved for a loan. It's important you do this for two reasons:

1. If you know the price range you can afford, you're unlikely to waste time and spin your wheels looking at homes you can't afford.

2. When you have a loan pre-approval letter (Figure 1-1) and find your dream home, you'll be in a position to make a quick decision and a fast offer. If you love the home, chances are others will too.

If you're already a homeowner, are planning to do some upgrading or remodeling, and need to tap into your equity to finance it, shopping around for the best deal is just as important as when you bought your home.

Whether you are buying or refinancing, in this chapter you'll learn:

• What leverage, appreciation, and equity mean and why they're important

• What it takes to qualify for a mortgage

• How to apply for an Energy Efficient Mortgage (EEM).

- How to shop for an eco-friendly mortgage lender
- How to compare loans to make sure you get the best deal

Figure 1-1. Loan Pre-Approval Letter.

ARBOR CAPITAL MORTGAGE, INC.

October 30, 2007

RE: John and Jill Doe
Mortgage pre-Approval letter

John and Jill Doe have applied for a mortgage loan with Arbor Capital Mortgage, Inc. We have evaluated their credit reports, verified their incomes, employment history, sources of down payment, and closing costs.

The Doe loan application has been reviewed by an underwriter and they have been pre-approved for a $285,000 mortgage subject to the following conditions:

1. Maximum purchase price of $285,000.
2. Home to appraise for at least the purchase price.
3. Interest rate at time of lock-in not to exceed 6.75 percent.
4. A clean title report on property by an accredited title company.
5. No significant change in assets or employment.
6. Final underwriting and quality control approval.
7. HERS estimate of energy savings not less than $215 per month.

If you have any questions, please call me at 685-2505.

Blaine Rickford
President
Arbor Capital Mortgage, Inc.

921 E. Executive Park Drive, Suite A. Salt Lake City, UT 84117. - (801) 685-2505 - Fax (801) 685-2509

UNDERSTANDING LEVERAGE, APPRECIATION, AND EQUITY

If you're a first time homeowner, the following terms will help you understand mortgage-speak and the underpinnings of how home loans work. If you are looking to finance home improvements, you'll learn how much of your equity you can comfortably borrow.

Leverage has to do with how you use borrowed money and how a low down payment can control an asset worth many times the money you put down.

Leverage can be a double-edged sword, as we've experienced recently in collapsing housing markets. In these markets, buyers were tempted to choose *zero down, interest only,* or *variable rate loans*—in other words, loans that required no money down, charged interest due at regular intervals, or featured interest rates that could increase or decrease to keep pace with market conditions.

The optimistic thinking of these homebuyers is that they can ultimately sell or refinance and make a bundle from the increase in the value of their home, which will be worth many times more than their initial down payment investment.

If you put a $13,000 down payment on a $260,000 home, your down payment controls a $260,000 asset. If the home's value goes up to $315,000, your $13,000 investment will have grown to $55,000—a 323-percent return, thanks to leverage.

Unfortunately, as we've all seen from 2007's mortgage meltdown, there's a dark side to leverage. A cooling market with dropping home prices can catch homeowners with a leveraged loan they can't afford or can't refinance.

When a home's value increases, that's *appreciation*. In the previous example, the appreciation would be $55,000. If, on the other hand, the home decreases in value, that's *depreciation*.

Equity, another important term, is the difference between a home's current value and the balance of the loan, or loans. Equity can go up or down, depending on the local real estate market. If your loan balance is $220,000 and the home's value is $345,000, your equity is $125,000. Typically, a number of things can determine your home's value, such as:

- An appraisal from a state-licensed real estate appraiser

- The tax valuation the county assessor's office assigns your home for property tax purposes, as stated in the *tax valuation* form you get each year

- A Comparative Market Analysis (CMA) done by a Realtor®, that lists what similar homes in the area have sold for recently as well as those that are currently for sale

To further illustrate equity, suppose you were to talk to a mortgage lender about a *second mortgage* (or other loan in addition to your first mortgage) to upgrade your home's energy efficiency. The lender may be willing to loan you up to 90 percent of your equity. In our previous example, that would mean you could borrow 90 percent of $125,000, or $112,500, for your upgrades.

Lenders also like to use the term *loan-to-value (LTV)*. This is the percentage of your home's value that is mortgaged. If you were to buy a home with 10 percent down, the LTV would be 90 percent. As lenders tighten up what income ratios and credit scores you'll need to qualify for a loan, LTV becomes more important.

Not long ago in the free-wheeling days of mortgage lenders making bad loans and homeowners going along with unrealistic terms, it was possible to get loans of upwards of 125 percent LTV. That meant you would owe 25 percent more than your home's value. When home values were on the rise, lenders felt confident that the home's value would catch up with the loan in a short time. If you couldn't make the payment, you could always sell the home, pay them off, take your profit, and do it all over again.

QUALIFYING FOR A MORTGAGE

The first step in buying a home is to take a close look at your financial situation and ask yourself three questions:

1. **Is your job/career reasonably stable in the near future?** Most mortgages are for fifteen or thirty years, so you need the job stability or skills to make payments over the long term.

2. **Can you handle a commitment for making long-term monthly payments?** Mortgage payments are due on the first of every month, and if your income doesn't sync, you'll need to have a reserve. Many self-employed homeowners maintain a reserve to handle mortgage payments in these situations.

3. **What monthly house payment amount can you comfortably handle without putting yourself in a financial straightjacket?** This is something only you can answer. Too many homebuyers in the past few years have gotten into trouble with their mortgage lenders because they didn't take the time to understand the details of their loans.

Mortgage programs that you want to look at with caution include:

- Variable rate mortgages, which commonly start out with low interest rates but increase or reset every six months to two years, depending on the program

- Loans that offer a low teaser rate for the first few months then adjust upward to the current market interest rate, which is usually several percentage points higher

- Mortgages that have *prepayment penalties*, where the lender charges you for paying the loan off early. Typically, the penalty is for the first five years and can cost you 1 to 5 percent of the loan balance. Always ask the lender if the loan has a pre-payment penalty. If it does, continue shopping.

When the payment with a loan program can change over the term of the mortgage, ask the loan officer to print you a disclosure sheet that figures the worst- and best-case numbers.

Although most mortgage lenders work hard to put a loan together and get you the best possible terms, it's still the Wild West when it comes to mortgages. You have to do your homework and make sure you understand the terms before signing anything before or at closing.

Typically a mortgage broker's job is to take the credit and income data you provide and assemble it into a profile of you as a potential long-term borrower. Your broker shops your file to various investors by phone, fax, or e-mail. If you want to work only with eco-friendly programs, then your broker will limit his or her submissions to investors who support your goals.

Since the mortgage industry is highly competitive, investors are not alike in their rates and terms. A good mortgage broker will sift through the offers and negotiate the best deal possible on your file.

The investor who agrees to make you a loan based on the information you provided then sends a commitment to the mortgage broker. Sometimes conditional approvals are given, subject to additional information or documents, but once completed, the loan paperwork moves on to the closing agent.

Depending on the state you live in, closing is handled by a title company, attorney, or escrow company. Closing is when you sign the loan paperwork and pay the down payment you agreed on. Additional costs you agree to pay the lender and closing agent are called closing costs. These costs are detailed in the good faith estimate discussed in the section called Finding a Lender with the Best Deal. The entire loan process from offer to closing should take thirty days or less.

The Importance of Your Credit Score

Because most lending today is Internet-based, an accepted credit standard is needed to put everyone on the same page. As a result, credit scoring was developed and has become standard in the industry, though sometimes it's controversial and misunderstood.

FICO scoring, named after Fair, Isaac and Co., the California-based firm that developed the software, creates a computer-generated numerical grade (typically 400 to 850) that predicts a lender's risk in loaning you money. The higher the score, the better risk you are to get a loan for a car, house, or whatever.

For example, if you pay your bills on time and haven't maxed out your credit cards, you probably have a score in the 700s. However, if you have a few thirty-day late payments and your credit cards are nearing their limits, your score can drop to the 500 to 600 range.

Your FICO score can change from day to day as your creditors (mortgage lenders, banks, credit card issuers, or other credit sources) report to the credit bureaus on how well you meet the terms of your obligations.

Three companies, Equifax, Experian, and Trans Union, dominate the credit reporting business. Since these agencies use different models for credit scoring, it's common for a lender to use reports from all three to establish your credit worthiness. Because each reporting agency gets its information in a slightly different way, it's not uncommon for your credit score to differ between 20 and 50 points on each report.

That's not always a problem, because mortgage lenders typically update discrepancies or reconcile differences in reports to get a current picture of your credit for better (hopefully) or worse (unfortunately).

If there are problems, the lender may ask you to write a short letter to explain your side. Should you have to write one of these letters, keep it short and stick to the facts. Applicants sometimes get carried away and include their family history.

 Credit Tip

Variable rate loans (ARMs) typically start out a percentage point or two less than the current rate and are adjusted up or down according to the performance of a common financial index. Payment adjustment periods are typically every six months or yearly, but can be longer depending on the program.

ARMs can also have caps that limit the interest rate adjustment to no more than 1 or 2 percent per year or adjustment period.

If you would lose sleep over a mortgage payment that could go up, you would likely be more comfortable with a fixed rate.

Scores of 700 and above typically qualify you for the best interest rates and terms. If you have a credit score under 700, you may still be able to get a loan, but interest rates and closing costs are likely to be higher.

During the days of runaway sub-prime loans, it appeared lenders approved anyone who could fill out a loan application. They tied borrower's credit scores to the prevailing interest rate—those with lower scores had to pay higher interest rates—and added in variable or low introductory rates to make them more appealing. This resulted in many foreclosures when interest rates shot up and house payments soared after the adjustment periods. The lesson learned from this is that if you have a lower credit score, it's better to clean up your credit rating so that you can qualify for good interest rates and terms before buying a home.

For example, when homebuyers Rob and Susan applied for a $200,000 mortgage, they didn't think a couple of thirty-day late payments on their two maxed-out Visa cards would cause a problem. But when their loan officer called asking about a two-year old medical collection account they had forgotten about, the situation started to look grim. Although Rob and Susan thought their insurance company was supposed to pay the bill, they never took the time to follow up and ignored several statements from the clinic. After about four months, the clinic sent the account to a collection agency that reported it to the credit bureau, and Rob and Susan's credit score took a big hit. Consequently, they were not able to get the home on terms they could comfortably handle.

Improving Your Credit Score

Unfortunately, quick fixes, magic potions, or silver bullets won't transform a credit rating from bad to good. Scammers tell you that, for a fee, they can fix a bad rating fast. Don't fall for it; it's wasted money. An experienced mortgage lender can work with you to up your credit score legitimately, and it won't cost you.

However, there are several things most lenders agree can improve your overall credit score:

- Pay down debt on high-interest credit cards as much as possible. Getting your balances below half of the card's limit is best.

- Pay off and close out small, seldom-used accounts. Too much credit can sometimes lower your score because lenders feel that you can tap these accounts after a loan is approved.

- Limit the number of inquires on your credit. A flurry of credit checks can raise a red flag and cost you points.

- Avoid accepting pre-approved credit cards and extended financing offers until after you close.

- Avoid switching insurance companies or refinancing. These often bring on new inquiries.

- Of course, the best credit builder is making your payments on time. Late payments (thirty days or more) will slash points from your FICO score.

- Your payment history from the past two years has the most weight, and prior problems, such as a bankruptcy, can have less impact after two years. You need to clearly show that you've cleaned up your act and made all monthly payments on time

If your credit is shaky, the best strategy is to work with a reputable mortgage lender. Such lenders are usually willing to go over your credit reports and work up a list of areas that you can improve or problems that you need to correct. Lenders know the credit system and what it takes to qualify you for the best mortgage rates.

Correcting Credit Problems

Occasionally, problems arise from errors, misreporting, or outdated information. You can usually clear these problems on your own, without paying the hefty fees scammers try to charge you.

If you have a disagreement with a credit agency, you have the right to question their information. *The Fair Credit Reporting Act (FCRA)* provides effective avenues to resolve reporting disputes. This isn't a way to erase legitimate late pays from your report or to turn bad credit into good, but it is a legal avenue to remove errors. For more info on credit reporting, go to: www.pueblo.gsa.gov/cic_text/money/fair-credit/fair-crd.htm

It's usually best to work closely with mortgage lenders to remove or correct errors in your credit report. They are professionals who know their way around the credit-reporting arena.

Determining How Big a House Payment You Can Afford

The biggest mistake most homebuyers and remodelers make is to start looking at homes or drawing up plans before they talk to a lender. It's important to get your financing approved up-front so that everyone is dealing with what is achievable, as opposed to what would be ideal. Often, home buyers and remodelers learn that their tastes may be a Mercedes S-550, but their income suggests they should be shopping for a Kia Rio.

 Credit Tip

If you're planning on buying a home that you want to remodel into a green or eco-friendly project, you may want to estimate how much it will cost you up-front. If you max out your income with mortgage payments, completing your eco-project may be more difficult.

Although each lender can have a slightly different focus, most like to keep income-to-debt ratios close to the following two percentages:

• Typically, total debt plus the mortgage payment, including principal, interest, taxes, and insurance, known as your total house payment, or PITI, should not exceed 36 to 42 percent of your pre-tax income. In some instances, if the borrower has a great credit score or exceptional assets, the lender may agree to go higher. However, as a consumer you have to look at your situation and decide what works for you, rather than let a lender pressure you. Some homeowners can handle 50 percent or more of their income going to a house payment and other debt, while others may be unable to handle 35 percent.

•   Your total house payment (PITI) should not exceed 28 to 30 percent of your monthly income before taxes, or gross income. Again, you have to take charge of your situation and stay within what you know will work for you. Becoming a slave to a house payment is not much fun.

Aaron and Ronda's application is a good example of how this works. When they decided to buy a home, they began by totaling their pay stubs. Before deductions, their income came to $7,240 a month. Next they added up their monthly payments: $545 for a car payment, $150 Visa and $75 Discover card payments, and $190 for a student loan. Their debt total: $960.

Due to Aaron and Ronda's good credit score, stable job history, and their ability to pay a 10 percent down payment, their mortgage lender told them they would be able to afford 41 percent of their income minus their debts. Doing the math, 0.41 x $7,240 equals $2,968.40; subtracting monthly debts of $960 leaves $2,004.40 (28 percent) as their maximum total mortgage payment. This includes interest, principal, taxes, homeowner's insurance, and *mortgage insurance premiums (MIP)*.

🏠 Number Crunching

Investing in an inexpensive financial calculator allows you to crunch the numbers to discover how different interest rates and down payments affect your monthly payment. TI, Casio, and Sharp models are available from any office supply outlet.

Calculated Industries has several models that you can order online at www.calculated.com and www.templatezone.com/financial-calculator-software.php has a great program that works with Microsoft Excel.

MIP is an insurance policy that insures the lender against having to foreclose. It's required by most lenders when the down payment is less than 20 percent. Typically, the fee is 0.50 to 0.75 percent of the loan amount and is based on your down payment. In other words, if you can come up with at least 20 percent down, you'll save yourself a hefty monthly MIP fee. When you pay the loan down below the 80-percent range, lenders are supposed to drop the MIP coverage. However, when home prices inflate, many borrowers take a short cut and refinance to lower interest rates with an 80 percent loan-to-value, eliminating the MIP in the process.

Back to Aaron and Ronda: Assume that 20 percent of the payment goes toward taxes, insurance, and MIP: $2,008 x 0.20 equals $402. When you subtract that figure from $2,008, $1,606 remains, which determines the price range that Aaron and Ronda have to work with. Using a financial calculator and keying in a payment of $1,606 at 6.50 percent interest for 30 years (360 months) yields $254,087 as the amount of the loan. Since the buyers are putting $26,000 down, that's added in, for a total purchase price of $280,087.

If it's a strong *buyer's market*—if there are a lot of homes on the market and sellers are motivated—Aaron and Ronda may look for homes in the $300,000 price range, but their offer will need to be around $280,000. As you'll see in the next section, though, the maximum house price may increase when you factor in an *energy efficient mortgage.*

GETTING AN ENERGY EFFICIENT MORTGAGE

Now that you've got a good idea about what it takes to qualify for a mortgage and are able to determine how much you can afford, the next step is to find a mortgage that will help you realize your goal of becoming more energy efficient.

More lenders are becoming environmentally conscious and offer discounts and programs for energy efficient homes and upgrades. Some offer programs that help you qualify for larger loans because the estimated monthly energy savings increase your ability to make a larger monthly payment. Other options allow you to roll the cost of making a home more energy efficient into the loan. For example, adding the $50 a month gained from energy savings to your mortgage payment equals $600 a year, and that increases borrowing power on a 30-year mortgage by $10,000. This can make the difference in getting the home and the location you want.

The *Energy Efficient Mortgages Program (EEM)* is set up to help homebuyers and homeowners save money on their utility bills by allowing them to finance the cost of adding energy efficient features to new or existing homes. The advantages of this program are that you can:

- Apply energy savings to qualify for a larger mortgage

- Remodel your home to make it more energy efficient. EEMs can also be used with HUD's Title I Home Improvement Loan program.

- Refinance to make your home more attractive and competitive when selling

- Upgrade outdated and inefficient heating and cooling systems

- Roll energy upgrades into the purchase mortgage when buying a home. This works especially well with *FHA 203(k) programs*, which allow a buyer to roll the fix-up costs into the mortgage.

- Use an EEM with *FHA's Section 203(h) program*, a special program for homeowners rebuilding in federally declared disaster areas.

- Choose from many lenders when shopping around, because most mortgage lenders can make loans covered by EEM programs

- Use EEMs with conventional, FHA, and VA loans, as well as with most state housing authority programs

- Increase the potential resale value of your home

- Make your house more affordable in a competitive market

 More EEM Information

www.pueblo.gsa.gov/cic_text/housing/energy_mort/energy-mortgage.htm,

www.hud.gov/offices/hsg/sfh/title/ti_abou.cfm,

www.hes.lbl.gov/hes/makingithappen/no_regrets/eemhowtoget.gif

www.eren.doe.gov

www.info@ase.org

Obtaining a Home Energy Ratings Systems Report

Once you've found a home you want to buy (whether new or existing) or you're ready to refinance your existing mortgage, you'll need to get an energy audit or a Home Energy Ratings Systems (HERS) report, described below, from a *certified energy rater*. The mortgage lender should have a list of approved inspectors. The cost for a report is usually between $300 and $800.

The inspector rates the project with a score between 1 and 100: the higher the score, the greater the energy efficiency. A HERS report will include:

- The existing energy rating score of the home
- Recommended energy upgrades
- Cost estimates for the upgrades, projected annual energy savings, and the upgrades' payback time
- What the energy rating score should be with the upgrades installed
- Estimated monthly and annual energy savings

If the HERS report shows that by upgrading you'll save money and recoup the costs within a reasonable time, then you have a doable project. Some of the items the inspector looks at when totaling up the home's score are:

1. Window energy efficiency; in cold climates, older single pane window replacement will be at the top of the list
2. The home's shell insulation efficiency
3. The age and efficiency of the furnace and air conditioner
4. The condition of the ductwork and insulation
5. The solar orientation of the home and how it effects heat gain and loss
6. The age and condition of the appliances
7. Insulation in the basement or crawlspace

When the loan officer gets the HERS report back, he or she determines how much money can be added to the appraisal (maximum 15 percent of the home's value) to finance the upgrades and how it will impact your loan total. Typically, the monthly energy savings is credited to your qualifying ratios, as if additional income. One couple increased their mortgage loan by nearly $10,000 to cover the costs of adding insulation, replacing old single pane aluminum windows with vinyl double panes, and adding a new water heater. The improvements were completed within a week of closing, and the new owners are now saving about $200 a month on utility bills and have a more comfortable home.

Shopping for the Best EEM Deal

Once you've decided to apply for an EEM mortgage, the next step—an important one—is to shop around for the best deal. This section will give you the tools and skills to confidently shop for a mortgage lender and not get ripped off by high loan fees.

This is not to say that most lenders are looking to rip you off. Good lenders are professional and work hard to put your loan together quickly and make the experience enjoyable. Unfortunately, bad lenders cost you time, money, and frustration, because they don't have the resources or competence to do a good job.

Dan and Kaelynn found out the hard way about bad lenders when a relative pressured them to work with a friend in the mortgage business. They had found a cute bungalow close to their children's school that needed some upgrades, and they wanted to make an EEM-FHA offer with a four-week closing date.

The loan officer took their application and explained he would need a $300 credit and application fee to get started and would get back to them in a few days. Two weeks later, when Dan and Kaelynn hadn't heard from their lender, they called him several times. They got only a recorded message, so they left him messages. He never returned their calls.

Finally, in the third week, Kaelynn got their lender's home number from their relative and called him. They got a big shock when he told them that his company was not an FHA-approved lender and didn't handle EEM programs, so he couldn't do a loan for them. However, he said, they were not entitled to the $300 refund of the application fees because it had been spent on a credit report and other fees.

Dan and Kaelynn ended up losing this home purchase; the sellers had a backup offer and refused to extend the closing date. Fortunately, Dan and Kaelynn were able to get their *earnest money deposit* back that they had included with their offer, because it was subject to financing.

Lesson learned: Never pay more than the credit report fee, which is normally $40 to $75, up front. When the credit report comes back and it appears the loan is a go, at that point order and pay for the appraisal, HERS inspection, and other required fees.

It can be sticky, but if a lender is a relative or friend, let them compete with other companies for your business. The old saying about the pitfalls of doing business with friends and relatives applies even more to mortgage lending, since it's such an emotionally charged situation.

Steps to Getting an EEM

To get an EEM, you need to take the following steps:

- Once you've decided on a mortgage lender, tell him or her you want an EEM loan.

- Have a HERS inspection done on the home you're planning to buy, or on your existing home if it's a refinance. You may have to write in the purchase contract that the deal is subject to an energy inspection. Most states' home purchase forms have checkboxes or fill-in lines for various inspections. You'll have to pay the inspection fee up-front, but some lenders allow you to include it in the loan.

- Once you have the inspection paperwork, decide which cost-effective improvements you want and find a contractor to do the work. You may want to collect three bids and screen the contractors by looking at past jobs and checking out their references.

- From the HERS paperwork, the lender will determine what funds are needed, and these go into an escrow.

- When the loan closes, the contractor is given the go-ahead to do the upgrades. Upon completion, the contractor is paid from the funds in escrow.

Finding a Lender with the Best Deal

A good strategy for finding a lender is asking for referrals from friends and coworkers who have recently bought or refinanced a home. Other good sources include Realtors and people who work for title companies.

Once you have narrowed your search to a short list of three mortgage companies, ask each of them to work up a *good faith estimate* (GFE) based on your financial information. A GFE offers the borrower an approximation of the closing costs, down payment balances, prepaid expenses, and other charges that must be addressed at closing. The best tool available to compare fees in order to determine which company is offering you the best deal, it is like a balance sheet. The loan costs are itemized, with a total for each section and a grand total at the bottom. This allows you to study the GFEs from competing lenders and narrow down the best deal. (See Figure 1-2.)

Figure 1-2. Good Faith Estimate Form.

GOOD FAITH ESTIMATE

Applicants:	Application No:
Property Addr:	Date Prepared: **10/12/2007**
Prepared By: **Home Loan Corporation Ph. 801-294-4663**	Loan Program: **Conv 30 yr fixed**
130 N. Main, Bountiful, UT 84010	

The information provided below reflects estimates of the charges which you are likely to incur at the settlement of your loan. The fees listed are estimates - actual charges may be more or less. Your transaction may not involve a fee for every item listed. The numbers listed beside the estimates generally correspond to the numbered lines contained in the HUD-1 settlement statement which you will be receiving at settlement. The HUD-1 settlement statement will show you the actual cost for items paid at settlement.

Total Loan Amount $ **270,000**   Interest Rate: **6.500** %   Term: **360 / 360** mths

800	ITEMS PAYABLE IN CONNECTION WITH LOAN:			PFC S F POC
801	Loan Origination Fee	1.000 %	$ 2,700.00	✓
802	Loan Discount			
803	Appraisal Fee		400.00	
804	Credit Report		28.50	
805	Lender's Inspection Fee			
808	Mortgage Broker Fee			
809	Tax Related Service Fee		100.00	
810	Processing Fee		100.00	
811	Underwriting Fee		100.00	
812	Wire Transfer Fee		20.00	
	Flood Zone Certification		20.00	
	Document Preparation		175.00	

1100	TITLE CHARGES:		PFC S F POC
1101	Closing/Escrow Fee:	$ 150.00	✓
1105	Document Preparation Fee	50.00	
1106	Notary Fees		
1107	Attorney Fees		
1108	Title Insurance:	940.00	
	Endorsements to Title Policy	55.00	

1200	GOVERNMENT RECORDING & TRANSFER CHARGES:		PFC S F POC
1201	Recording Fees:	$ 75.00	
1202	City/County Tax/Stamps:		
1203	State Tax/Stamps:		

1300	ADDITIONAL SETTLEMENT CHARGES:		PFC S F POC
1302	Pest Inspection	$	
	Courier fees	20.00	

	Estimated Closing Costs		**4,933.50**

900	ITEMS REQUIRED BY LENDER TO BE PAID IN ADVANCE:				PFC S F POC
901	Interest	for	15 days @ $ 48.7500 / day $	731.25	✓
902	Mtg Ins. Premium				
903	Hazard Ins. Premium			540.00	
904					
905	VA Funding Fee				

1000	RESERVES DEPOSITED WITH LENDER:			PFC S F POC
1001	Hazard Ins. Premium	2 mths @ $ 45.00 / mth $	90.00	
1002	Mtg Ins. Premium Reserves	mths @ $ 117.00 / mth		
1003	School Tax	mths @ $ / mth		
1004	Taxes & Assessment Reserves	2 mths @ $ 200.00 / mth	400.00	
1005	Flood Insurance Reserves	mths @ $ / mth		
		mths @ $ / mth		
		mths @ $ / mth		

	Estimated Prepaid Items/Reserves	**1,761.25**
		6,694.75

TOTAL ESTIMATED SETTLEMENT CHARGES

TOTAL ESTIMATED FUNDS NEEDED TO CLOSE:				TOTAL ESTIMATED MONTHLY PAYMENT:	
Purchase Price/Payoff (+)	300,000.00	New First Mortgage(-)		Principal & Interest	1,706.58
Loan Amount (-)	270,000.00	Sub Financing(-)		Other Financing (P & I)	
Est. Closing Costs (+)	4,933.50	New 2nd Mtg Closing Costs(+)		Hazard Insurance	45.00
Est. Prepaid Items/Reserves (+)	1,761.25			Real Estate Taxes	200.00
Amount Paid by Seller (-)				Mortgage Insurance	117.00
				Homeowner Assn. Dues	
				Other	
Total Est. Funds needed to close			36,694.75	**Total Monthly Payment**	2,068.58

These estimates are provided pursuant to the Real Estate Settlement Procedures Act of 1974, as amended (RESPA). Additional information can be found in the HUD Special Information Booklet, which is to be provided to you by your mortgage broker or lender, if your application is to purchase residential real property and the lender will take a first lien on the property. The undersigned acknowledges receipt of the booklet "Settlement Costs," and if applicable the Consumer Handbook on ARM Mortgages.

Applicant	Date	Applicant	Date

Calyx Form - gfe2.frm (09/07)

TRUTH-IN-LENDING DISCLOSURE STATEMENT
(THIS IS NEITHER A CONTRACT NOR A COMMITMENT TO LEND)

Applicants:

Property Address:

Application No:

Prepared By: **Home Loan Corporation**
130 N. Main
Bountiful , UT 84010
801-294-4663

Date Prepared: **10/12/2007**

ANNUAL PERCENTAGE RATE	FINANCE CHARGE	AMOUNT FINANCED	TOTAL OF PAYMENTS
The cost of your credit as a yearly rate	The dollar amount the credit will cost you	The amount of credit provided to you or on your behalf	The amount you will have paid after making all payments as scheduled
7.254 %	$ 390,074.16	$ 266,418.75	$ 656,492.91

☐ REQUIRED DEPOSIT: The annual percentage rate does not take into account your required deposit
PAYMENTS: Your payment schedule will be:

Number of Payments	Amount of Payments **	When Payments Are Due	Number of Payments	Amount of Payments **	When Payments Are Due	Number of Payments	Amount of Payments **	When Payments Are Due
		Monthly Beginning:			Monthly Beginning:			Monthly Beginning:
359	1,823.58	12/01/2007						
1	1,827.69	11/01/2037						

☐ DEMAND FEATURE: This obligation has a demand feature.
☐ VARIABLE RATE FEATURE: This loan contains a variable rate feature. A variable rate disclosure has been provided earlier.

CREDIT LIFE/CREDIT DISABILITY: Credit life insurance and credit disability insurance are not required to obtain credit, and will not be provided unless you sign and agree to pay the additional cost.

Type	Premium	Signature	
Credit Life		I want credit life insurance.	Signature:
Credit Disability		I want credit disability insurance.	Signature:
Credit Life and Disability		I want credit life and disability insurance.	Signature:

INSURANCE: The following insurance is required to obtain credit:
☐ Credit life insurance ☐ Credit disability ☑ Property insurance   ☐ Flood insurance
You may obtain the insurance from anyone you want that is acceptable to creditor
☐ If you purchase   ☐ property   ☐ flood insurance from creditor you will pay $ for a one year term.
SECURITY: You are giving a security interest in:
☑ The goods or property being purchased   ☐ Real property you already own.
FILING FEES: $ 70.00
LATE CHARGE: If a payment is more than **15** days late, you will be charged   **5.000** % of the payment
PREPAYMENT: If you pay off early, you
☐ may   ☑ will not   have to pay a penalty.
☐ may   ☑ will not   be entitled to a refund of part of the finance charge.
ASSUMPTION: Someone buying your property
☐ may   ☐ may, subject to conditions   ☑ may not   assume the remainder of your loan on the original terms.
See your contract documents for any additional information about nonpayment, default, any required repayment in full before the scheduled date and prepayment refunds and penalties
☐ * means an estimate   ☐ all dates and numerical disclosures except the late payment disclosures are estimates.

* * NOTE: The Payments shown above include reserve deposits for Mortgage Insurance (if applicable), but exclude Property Taxes and Insurance.

THE UNDERSIGNED ACKNOWLEDGES RECEIVING A COMPLETED COPY OF THIS DISCLOSURE.

_____   _____
(Applicant)   (Date)   (Applicant)   (Date)

_____   _____
(Applicant)   (Date)   (Applicant)   (Date)

_____
(Lender)   (Date)

Calyx Form - til.hp (02/95)

In Figure 1-2, p.2, you'll find a box labeled *Annual Percentage Rate (APR)*. This is the interest rate you're charged for the loan including the closing costs. For example, one lender may charge 6.50 percent interest and $4,900 in closing costs. Another lender may charge 6.25 percent interest, but $5,600 in closing costs. It can be confusing to know what the bottom line really is. Fortunately, this is where the APR comes in: The least costly loan will have the lowest APR. This is the key to determining the best deal.

Avoiding Garbage Fees

Like any other businessperson, a mortgage broker can survive only if making a profit. That's fine, but as a savvy consumer you don't what that profit to be any bigger than it has to be. You have to be vigilant to avoid padded and unnecessary costs, called *garbage fees*, creeping into your loan. Sometimes the line between the two becomes blurry, and the only way you can tell is by comparing fees from several lenders.

For instance, one lender may charge a 1 percent origination fee ($1,000 on a $100,000 mortgage), a typical fee charged for getting you the loan. Suppose a mortgage broker increases this fee to 1.5 percent, or $1,500. This is certainly not illegal or even unethical, but why should you pay more than you have to? By comparing fees, you'll likely find other lenders charging 1 percent, or perhaps only 0.5 percent if they're hungry and trying to build up their mortgage volume. Typically, though, the normal fees, if you exclude an origination fee, will run from $600 to $975.

 Consumer Tip

Keep the good faith estimate from your lender handy. Ask the title company or closing agent to fax or deliver you copies of the closing statements (HUDs; See Negotiating Lender Fees below) to compare with the GFE before going to closing.

Garbage fees are sometimes added in at the last minute, and it's better to contest these before sitting down at the closing table.

Negotiating Lender Fees

You don't want to be fooled by lenders who create a package with low teaser rates and then make up for it with additional fees. The only way to determine how good a deal you're getting is to compare good faith estimates side by side. Don't hesitate to question fees and negotiate a reduction or waiver.

Few buyers take the time to understand these fees because they are intimidated by the whole process. Unfortunately, since few buyers question them or seem to care, a why-not-add-them-in attitude becomes common with many bankers.

The best time to question and negotiate fees is soon after you get your good faith estimates. You want to have everything settled before closing day and not create a pressure situation that could delay your closing at the last minute.

Also, whenever you and the lender agree to changes, always get them in writing, including a revised GFE. This is your best defense against last-minute fee add-ons.

The last step before closing is to request that the title company or whoever closes the loan fax you copies of the closing statements that break down your closing costs (government-required forms) called HUDS a few hours before closing. But that rarely happens. More commonly, the closing agency may not get the loan package until just before you come in to close. If that's the case, take a few minutes to sit down and go over the HUD statements alone before closing. Take notes, and if you have questions, bring them up when you and the person closing the loan go over the statements. This is important, because if there are fees or other costs that are different from your GFE, you want to take care of it before you get to the closing table if at all possible. If you can't, then don't worry about it. Statements can be changed and reprinted until they're satisfactory. Don't let a closer tell you the statements can't be changed. They may have to get on the phone to the lender or have them fax something over. But that's fine; you're the consumer and you want it done right.

One couple, Carlos and Hilda, decided they needed to be more informed the second time around, when they decided to refinance with an EEM and do some badly needed upgrades. This time they were determined to know what they were paying for, so they decided to get GFEs from their current lender and two others before committing.

Comparing the estimates line by line, Carlos and Hilda found that their current lender was charging them a $300 processing fee and 1.25 percent loan origination fee. The two other lenders were charging only 1 percent for the origination fee, and while one had no processing fee, the other had a fee of only $125—a considerable savings over what their current lender was offering.

Totaling all the costs revealed that Carlos and Hilda's current lender was the most expensive on the list by $862.50. However, he was charging 5.90 percent interest and the other lenders were quoting 6.0 percent. Doing a little math, Hilda calculated that the difference in monthly payments between 5.9 percent and 6.0 percent was $14.43, or $173.16 a year. Dividing the $14.43 payment difference into $862.50 yielded almost 60 months. That meant that if they didn't sell or refinance their home for five years, they would reach the break-even point. Not wishing to waste time haggling with their current lender, Carlos and Hilda decided to go with another lender whose bid they felt was more simple and straightforward.

Unfortunately, it didn't stay so simple. When the title company faxed the closing documents to Carlos at his office, he was out, and he didn't receive them until an hour before closing.

In doing a quick comparison between the closing statement and the good faith estimate, Carlos noticed that a $135 document preparation fee had been added. Not quite sure who to talk to, he called the title company and was referred to the mortgage lender. Finally getting through to the loan processor, Carlos had to do a little verbal arm twisting before the processor agreed that the fee was an error and that the paperwork would be corrected in time for the closing.

The bottom line is: If these homeowners hadn't done their homework, tracked their loan paperwork, and stayed on top of the entire process, they could have paid almost $1,000 more for their mortgage. Remember, it's a competitive world and you're the consumer. Any money you can save is better in your pocket than going to the bank's shareholders.

CASE STUDY: HOW IT ALL WORKS

First-time home buyers Rolf and Amber provide a good example of how an eco-friendly mortgage can come together. For years they had dreamed of finding a slightly run-down home that they could buy and restore using eco-friendly materials and making it energy efficient.

One morning when Amber was driving her son to school, she noticed an older home with a newly installed "for sale" sign and brochure box. She took one of the flyers and noticed that the home was not only in their price range, but that the agent specialized in green homes and renovation. Getting excited, she called the agent on her cell while parked in front of the home and set up a time to go through it when Rolf got off work.

It was exactly what Amber and Rolf were looking for and it was close to where they were renting. When Rolf brought up financing and explained that they didn't have a lot of money to make the home into what they wanted it to be, the agent told them not to worry. They would most likely qualify for an EEM loan, taking care of their biggest problem. However, their first step was to talk to a lender, get a loan pre-approval letter, and then write up an offer to present to the seller.

Lining up financing needed to be their first concern; otherwise, they would not know what they could afford. Rolf and Amber put together a list of several mortgage lenders from friends, coworkers, and ads. The first lender on their list reviewed their income and debt and told them, based on the information they had given her, they could borrow approximately $265,000. However, the lender was not familiar with EEMs and didn't appear interested in finding out, so that lender was crossed off the list.

After a morning spent calling other mortgage lenders, Amber identified three lenders who were familiar with EEM loans and were interested in talking to her and Rolf. The loan reps also promised to promptly e-mail good faith estimates of their programs.

That evening, Rolf and Amber and their Realtor spread out the three GFEs the lenders had e-mailed to them. In comparing them, they noticed that the loan fees varied widely. One had lower fees but a slightly higher interest rate, while another had a lower interest rate but higher fees. The third one they eliminated from consideration because it had both a higher interest rate and loan fees.

The difference between the other two estimates was about $1,400; the one with the lowest bid also, predictably, had the lowest APR. That made deciding which lender to go with an easy choice. The next step for the buyers was to make an appointment for a full application and pay a credit report fee.

By the time Rolf and Amber filled out the loan paperwork, the loan officer had gotten their credit scores and qualified them for a $267,000 loan. That figure would likely be adjusted upward when the HERS report came back and any energy savings were added in.

The last step was for the loan officer to print out a pre-approval letter for the buyers to attach to their real estate purchase offer, which they and their agent would write up. Since Rolf and Amber's agent had a lot of experience with EEM loans, he wrote in the offer that it was subject to a HERS audit and professional home inspection. This gave the buyers a way to cancel the offer if the audit or inspection found problems they couldn't deal with.

The buyers could also use the subject-to-home-inspection clause as a bargaining chip to motivate the owner to take care of any problems the inspector found. Typical problems buyer and sellers negotiate are roofing, foundation leaks or structural defects, plumbing, electrical wiring, and wall or floor damage. Sometimes the sellers agree to fix the problems rather than lose the sale. Other times they offer the buyers a cash or price reduction concession—whatever makes both sides happy.

In Rolf and Amber's case, the inspection revealed no serious problems that the planned upgrades wouldn't take care of. Still, the agent negotiated a $2,000 concession from the seller if the buyers would take the home as is.

The HERS reports came in with a high score, meaning that the upgrades would increase the home's energy efficiency considerably. The inspector estimated that it would cost about $18,000 to fund the window, insulation, and appliance upgrades.

With a sales price of $260,000 and the $18,000 HERS estimate, plus the seller's concession of $2,000, the buyers found that they had $20,000 up-front to begin creating their eco-friendly dream home.

Over the next two years Amber and Rolf added water-saving landscaping and started replacing vinyl flooring and nylon carpeting with resource-sustaining materials. For them it was a labor of love, with a long way to go before they're satisfied.

Finding homes to upgrade and eco-savvy brokers to help is sometimes a challenge. Chapter 2 offers tips and explains which traps to avoid when taking on this exciting challenge.

CHAPTER 2

FINDING AND WORKING WITH AN ECO-FRIENDLY AGENT

Once you've decided on a lender, completed the pre-approval routine, and received a letter pre-approving you for a specific dollar amount, you're ready to move on to the next step.

There are three ways you can proceed once you have loan approval:

1. Find and work with an agent who is trained or savvy in selling eco-friendly homes

2. Find a home on your own without the services of a professional

3. Both search on your own and use an agent

This chapter assumes that you're planning on buying a home that you can fix up to become environmentally responsible or one that's already upgraded. Building an eco-friendly home is covered in chapters 4 through 7, although the process of finding an eco-friendly agent remains the same.

Whether you're planning on buying or building an eco-friendly home, it's important to find an agent who shares your environmentally responsible vision. If that proves difficult—after all, not all agents are eco-friendly—you may need to take a proactive approach and do most of the house hunting, and even negotiating, on your own.

Frankly, it's a lot easier if you're able to use an eco-savvy realtor who is willing to work with you not only in finding that dream home, but in guiding you through the financing, negotiating, and offer stages.

In this chapter you'll learn:

- How to find a green agent who shares your vision
- What *agency* means and who agents represent in a transaction
- How to work with your agent to find green homes
- What to look for in green or fix-up homes before you commit
- How to shop for homes on your own if you can't find an agent

FINDING AN ECO-FRIENDLY AGENT

Realtors are professionals who you hire to help handle one of the most costly events in your life: buying and selling a home. As with looking for mortgage lenders, home inspectors, and brain surgeons, you want the best; you want someone who can be objective and whose expertise you can tap into. But most importantly, you want someone who has experience buying and selling eco-friendly homes.

Unfortunately, there are not yet a lot of agents who have the experience, savvy, or desire to work with environmentally sustainable or energy efficient real estate. The good news is that this is starting to change, as the National Association of Realtors (NAR) is now aware of the growing demand for green homes.

Many current eco-savvy real estate agents have come into sales from the building trades or from other green industries, hoping to fill a void and/or advance the green movement. Within this group you'll find agents, especially those who build or rehab homes, who have the knowledge and experience to guide you in fulfilling your dream of an environmentally sustainable home. The key is distinguishing such agents from among the many who don't have a clue.

Beginning Your Search

A good starting place for finding an eco-friendly real estate agent is www.ecobroker.com, the Web site for EcoBroker, an organization devoted to educating and certifying real estate brokers on the ins and outs of sustainable building. Their curriculum covers green building principles, Energy Star homes, and financing, as well as buying and selling green homes. According to John Beldock, CEO of EcoBroker, their goal is to get more clients into green homes by educating real estate brokers.

Go to EcoBroker's home page and key in your city and state to find a list of active members in your area. You may want to contact local brokers and set up meetings to find one who's a potential match with your personality and goals.

If there are no certified EcoBrokers in your area, you'll need to network and dig a little to find green agents who can help you realize your goals. Sources that can be fertile ground for networking include:

- Green builders in your area whose work you trust. Ask them if they know of a savvy agent. It's not uncommon for tradespeople, suppliers, and even builders to obtain real estate licenses.

- Referrals from people you know who have recently used a green agent to buy their homes.

- Building centers or suppliers who showcase environmentally sustainable materials. One company, The Green Building Center (www.green buildingcenter.net) in Salt Lake City, conducts a green home tour every year to show off innovations in rehab and new construction. These tours attract builders, agents, architects, suppliers, and others active in the green building arena.

- Architects, designers, and consultants who advertise in environmental publications.

- Mortgage lenders who advertise green financing.

- Salvage yards that cater to people who want to use recycled materials in their remodeling or new construction projects.

- Nurseries and landscape businesses that specialize in environmentally safe products and practices.

- Local environmental groups, which often leave flyers at businesses they support as well as libraries and other public places.

- Internet search engines, where you can key in such words as "green," "environment," "green building," or "green building materials" to lead you to local resources.

- Real estate agents: You can ask whether they know of any fellow agents who specialize in or are knowledgeable in green real estate.

- Attorneys and title people who do real estate closings.

Narrowing Your Search to an Agent Who Shares Your Dream

Once you've created a list of possible agents, pare it down to the three best candidates and set up appointments to meet with each of them. Sometimes the paring process is easy; agents may not return your calls or e-mails for a few days or not at all. These, of course, you can cross off the list.

In preparing for the interviews, it's important that you have two items ready:

1.   A letter from a mortgage lender on official letterhead stating the amount of a mortgage you can qualify for. This figure will be conservative, because you don't yet have the energy saving credits added in. You won't know that amount until you find the home and get a HERS report back. But it's better to work with the conservative figure, because you may find a home that requires increasing the amount to cover closing costs or improvements you want to roll into the loan.

2.   A checklist detailing what you're looking for in a home. This list, which you'll want to go over with the agent, will keep you focused on what you want to achieve and help you to decide whether the agent has the knowledge and experience to help you attain it. (See Figure 2-1.)

During your interviews, you should look for answers to the following questions before choosing an agent:

- What professional titles—such as EcoBroker or the National Association of Realtors' *Certified Residential Specialist (CRS)*—does the agent have? Licenses in related fields like building, landscape design, and architecture can also be a plus.

- Does the agent belong to any environmental or green organizations?

- Does the agent have the experience and technical skills to help you find the home you're looking for? In other words, if you want to install solar panels to achieve zero net energy use, can the agent direct you to the right resources?

Figure 2-1. Property Shopping Checklist.

Item	Description
Older Home	Home that can be rehabbed with recycled materials, upgraded energy features, and water-efficient landscaping.
Area	An older neighborhood that can support the improvements with increased value. Preferably an area that like-minded young professionals and environmentally concerned people are moving into.
Good Schools	Schools have a big impact on an area's value. Schools must have a good rating.
Structure	The home's foundation and structure need to be sound and not require extensive repairs.
Roof	Roof can need re-shingling, but not if so damaged that it requires tear-off and deck replacing, No serious water damage.
Exterior	Brick in good condition, wood siding that needs replacing ok, but no serious water damage.
Kitchen	Kitchen that has not been upgraded preferred.
Furnace/AC	Older furnace that has not been replaced recently preferred.
Site	Home needs to be oriented on the lot so solar panels can be mounted on the roof.
Landscaping	Bad condition, but reclaimable.
Price	$275,000 to $290,000
Concessions to seek	$4,500 to $6,500 closing costs, possibly additional costs for repairs.

- Has the agent been in the business long enough to know the local real estate market?

- Has the agent personally done any rehabbing? Does he or she share your enthusiasm on the importance of going green?

- Does the agent seem responsible? Advise any agent you're considering that prompt communication is important. With current technology, when you leave a message there's no excuse for an agent not to get back to you within an hour or two. If you reach voice mail every time you call and he or she is slow to get back to you, seriously consider going with someone else.

- Does the agent have access to the *Multiple Listing Service (MLS)* database (see Working with Your Agent to Find Green Properties for more) and know how to use it? Often, success finding the right property depends on how fast your agent picks up on new listings posted to the MLS.

- Do you feel that you are compatible with the agent? The home buying experience can become intense and emotional. If personalities clash, that can detract from finding the home you're looking for. It's better to find another agent than try to muddle through with a bad fit.

Unfortunately, there are a lot of real estate agents who aren't competent. You may have a licensed relative or friend who would be upset if you don't use him or her as your agent; for many regular homebuyers, using Aunt Molly, who just got her real estate license, to find a home can work out. But if you want to go the green route, you'll save yourself a lot of time and bucks if you go the extra mile to find a professional who specializes in environmentally sustainable homes. It's far better to explain to your agent friends or relatives why you need a specialist and take the heat than to stumble around trying to put a deal together with an agent who thinks green is just another color.

The Buyer's Agency: Who Does the Agent Represent?

No matter what agent you decide to work with, *agency* is something you need to be aware of. Most state real estate agencies take disclosure very seriously and require agents to disclose in writing whether they work for the buyer, seller, or both.

Basically, agency is a *fiduciary relationship* created when an agent agrees to work with a buyer or seller and enters into a written agreement pledging trust and confidence. For sellers, this performance relationship is created by the listing agreement. For buyers, however, there are more options:

- A buyer agency relationship can be created when a buyer finds a home and signs a purchase offer and agency disclosure forms.
- A buyer can agree to work with an agent; both sign a buyer agency agreement before they begin shopping for a home.
- A buyer can work with an agent who is also working with sellers in a limited agency agreement.

A buyer can choose to work with an agent in two ways, exclusively and non-exclusively. *Exclusive agency* means you agree to work only with that agent for an agreed upon period of time. For example, if you happen to see a home advertised for sale in a local environmental magazine and you go look at it and decide to make an offer, you're bound by the contract to have your agent write the offer.

The advantage of an exclusive agreement is that your agent will be motivated to work harder for you, knowing his or her efforts won't be wasted. Nevertheless, it's a good idea to have in writing that you can cancel the agreement by giving written notice. You'll still be bound to that agent for any properties previously shown you. But you won't be locked in with an agent that's not doing a good job.

Non-exclusive agency means you are not bound to an exclusive agent, but you must use the agent who shows you a property if you decide to make on offer on it. You can sign a non-exclusive agreement with as many agents as you want. But that can be counterproductive, because few agents are likely to take you seriously. It's best to go exclusively with one agent who you feel can do the job, as loyalty is usually a two-way street.

Before you sign any agency agreement, make sure the time frame for the agent getting a commission if you buy a home she shows you is not more than sixty days. This is important if, for some reason, you change agents and later decide to make an offer on a listing the previous agent showed you. Some agents ask for six months coverage, but that's excessive. If an agent is doing a good job, limiting this time frame won't be a problem.

Buyer agency forms vary from state to state, but the basics are similar and cover the following:

- An agent representing a homebuyer must have a written agency agreement defining the scope of the agency. In many states, approved forms are required.

- A buyer's agent works on behalf of the buyers and owes them his or her loyalty.

- The agent should not disclose any information that could weaken the buyer's bargaining position.

- The agent is responsible for and must account for all earnest money deposits in the trust account.

- The buyer's agent has an obligation to disclose to the seller and other agents upon initial contact that they have a buyer's agency agreement.

Of course, an agency agreement does not permit the agent to misrepresent your financial condition or ability to perform when presenting an offer. In other words, the agent can't lie and say you're pre-approved for a mortgage when you're not.

When an agent represents both buyer and seller it's called *dual* or *limited agency*. There is some controversy regarding dual agency. Because an agent who acts for both the buyer and seller is in a contradictory position, he or she must be neutral and cannot disclose any information that will harm either side's bargaining position. Some brokers feel the potential liability is so great that they will insist you find another agent to represent you if you're interested in a property he or she is listing.

Other brokers, however, don't have a problem with dual agency and feel comfortable representing both sides and taking care not to say anything that will compromise either the buyer's or seller's bargaining positions. In most cases, both sides end up happy with the results.

In reality, most problems associated with dual agency have related to the agent's failure to properly disclose in writing that he or she was working for both parties. State real estate regulators consider agents' failure to disclose exactly who they represent one of the cardinal sins.

There's an emerging concept called *transaction-brokerage* that some feel insulates the agent from potential conflicts of interest. A transaction-broker works with the consumer without establishing an agency relationship. In effect, the agent becomes a facilitator, working with either a buyer or seller to put the deal together. The goal of this option is to limit liability for the agent and the seller, as well as give consumers a choice if they don't want to be represented by an agent.

From the consumer's point of view, agency disclosure is a plus. It puts agents under the spotlight to be sure they disclose who they represent in a transaction and allows buyers the same representation sellers get from their listing agent.

WORKING WITH YOUR AGENT TO FIND GREEN PROPERTIES

Before you hit the road looking for homes you can upgrade, it's important to create an inspection worksheet similar to the one in Figure 2-2 to keep

Figure 2-2. Property Inspection Checklist.

Item	Pros and cons
Location	
Results of a walk through the neighborhood	
Schools	
Commuting distance	
Proximity to shopping and areas of interest.	
Home style	
Exterior condition	
Curb appeal	
Roof	
Furnace and water heater	
Potential for energy-saving upgrades	
Garage/carport	
Kitchen	
Appliances	
Family room	
Bedrooms	
Storage	
Basement	
Yard	
Work or updates needed	
Seller concessions to ask for	
Resale potential	
Estimated cost to rehab	$
Average cost of homes in the area	$
Estimated value of home after rehabbing.	$

you focused on what's important. You and your agent should have already reviewed your shopping list together during your interview and be on the same page as to your goals.

Sources for finding green homes or homes that can be upgraded to environmental sustainability can be challenging, since this concept is just starting to gain momentum across the country.

The *Multiple Listing Service (MLS)* is a database, owned by Realtors, of homes for sale, where member offices place their listings. When you work with a Realtor, he or she has access to the listings of all the member offices. That means a member agent can show you any house on the MLS and write offers and negotiate on your behalf.

Although the MLS is a giraffe among mice as far as the number of homes for sale go, it's by no means the only source, and may not even be the best source, in your area for finding existing green homes.

Even though the MLS database has a huge number of properties for sale, its current data fields for inputting green entries are few, leaving the remarks section of property listings as the default place to convey a home's environmental and energy saving features. In addition, sifting through hundreds, if not thousands, of listings by reading the remarks section can become tedious.

Also, in most areas the eco-friendly housing market is small enough that the majority of builders, architects, serious rehabbers, agents, and suppliers know who's who and what's happening in the area. If your agent specializes in green homes, chances are that he or she knows them, too, and can network for you.

Many homebuyers, especially first timers, who want a green home need to find a home they can rehab in order to achieve their dreams. As previously covered, many government loan programs and energy credits are making a green rehab a great way to go. All it takes is a plan and determination to make it happen.

In one case, two brothers, Ron and Andrew, dreamed of finding a home in a highly sought-after area near a university hospital and rehabbing it into a green home. They drove through the neighborhoods regularly looking for new "For Sale" signs before the houses appeared on the MLS.

Late one afternoon as Andrew turned down one of the streets in the area, he noticed an agent pulling a "For Sale" sign out of his car's trunk. He immediately pulled over and asked the agent the asking price. Andrew told him was already working with an agent but would like to take a look at the inside.

The owner had just moved into an assisted-living center, and the family wanted to sell the home in its present condition, or *as is*, because it hadn't been upgraded in two decades. It was a perfect opportunity. Andrew made a quick call to his agent and had her come over and write up an offer on the spot, to the delight of the listing agent.

Ron and Andrew rehabbed the home with mostly recycled and renewable materials and replaced the old, inefficient appliances, furnace, and air conditioner with Energy Star-rated units. They also replaced the windows with Energy Star-rated double-pane windows and upgraded the insulation.

It took five months of labor and $60,000 for the brothers to complete the renovation. They then planted their own "For Sale" sign on the lawn and quickly sold it to a single doctor moving in to work at the nearby university hospital. After subtracting the purchase price and renovation costs, Ron and Andrew netted close to $97,000 on their first project. In their next renovation, they plan to add a solar panel system to reduce energy use to near zero.

In another example, Chad and Brandi, a young couple with two small children under five, wanted a home in a certain school district and neighborhood. Their dream since college was to find a home they could remodel using environmentally sustainable materials to make it energy efficient.

Unfortunately, in the area they were interested in there were no homes on the market. But being resourceful, their agent put together a flyer with a picture of the buyer's family and a short letter outlining why they wanted to live in the area and asked anyone who was thinking of selling to call her. Chad, Brandi, and their agent spent one Saturday afternoon passing out about seventy-five flyers in the target neighborhood.

A week later, the agent got a call from a couple about to retire who had been thinking of downsizing and moving to a warmer state. The flyer prompted the sellers to decide that opportunity was knocking and that this might be the time to sell their home and move.

Upon inspecting the home, Chad and Brandi found it was just what they had been looking for. The home needed updating and the appliances needed replacing. An energy audit would reveal that many of the energy efficient upgrades they planned could be rolled into the mortgage, which would help to conserve their remodeling cash reserve for other upgrades they had in mind. They made what they thought was a fair offer considering the house's condition, and the sellers accepted it.

Of course, not all projects work out this smoothly or quickly. But it's amazing how often potential sellers are galvanized into action when they hear a qualified buyer is interested in the area, especially if the market is slow.

Buying a Fixer-Upper

Buying a rundown home and fixing it up to be energy efficient is a dream of many environmentally responsible buyers. You can have a lot fun and satisfaction going this route if sawdust and paint is your thing, but the waters are shark-infested. The key to not losing money is creating a step-by-step plan and following it.

It may be a cliché, but it's worth repeating: Location is everything. Homes in better locations increase in value more quickly and hold their value when the market is down. The last thing you want to do is buy a home and spend thousands of dollars making it energy efficient and environmentally friendly, only to find out in the end that it's overvalued for the neighborhood. You become an expert on an area by looking at homes for sale, visiting open houses, and comparing them with those that have recently sold. It won't take long before you understand property values and what you should offer when you discover a possibility. (See Figure 2-2.)

There are important dos for buying a fix-up property, including:

• Do choose the location carefully; go with the best area you can afford. It's better to buy a smaller home in a good area than a larger home in a not-so-good neighborhood. Also, check out the schools. Schools with good reputations help maintain and increase home values.

• Do ask your agent to run statistics on the area you're interested in. Note whether the values are going up or down and how long it's taking to sell homes.

• With the help of a contractor, do check out the property as thoroughly as possible and determine the upgrade costs. Get written bids on work you can't do yourself.

• Do be honest about whether you have the time and expertise to do what needs to be done. This is where the rubber meets the road. Make a list of what you can do and what you'll need to hire out. Get bids in hand and add in the material cost list for what you plan to do yourself. Add that total to the cost of the home. Then compare the total cost to the projected market value when you're finished.

• If possible, do make any offers contingent on a professional home inspection and a HERS report. These will cost you about $500 but will be worth it if they save you from an expensive mistake. If the reports come back revealing surprises, you can use them to renegotiate the price to cover repair costs.

Buying a Foreclosure to Rehab Can Be Tricky

You can sometimes buy a home that a bank has foreclosed on and get a good deal, but it can also be problematic.

Judy Morrell, a Salt Lake City rehabber for twenty years, has had a lot of success with foreclosed properties that she buys and her husband and sons fix up for resale. "You don't always have the option of inspecting the property beforehand," Morrell says, "so it's buyer beware. What you see is what you get." She also cautions that if you're not a pro, it's easy to get caught up in the bidding and pay too much. You must understand the location and the market value of the home you're bidding on and be able to walk away when others bid the price up beyond what you're willing to pay.

The best way to track foreclosure sales is to get a list of homes that have had a *Notice of Default* recorded. A Notice of Default is a notice recorded by the mortgage lender that the owner has defaulted on the payments. Usually the homeowner has 90 days to make arrangements with the bank or the home will go to a trustee's sale. This list is available from a title company or your county recorder's office.

Many people who specialize in foreclosure or distressed properties contact owners prior to the home going on the auction block and offer to buy out their equity. Here are some of the challenges of choosing this route:

• This is often an emotionally difficult time for the owners, and you have to tread lightly and approach them tactfully and with empathy. Often owners are in denial and refuse to face the reality that they are losing their home. Good people skills are a must in such cases.

• You need to work with a title company and get a preliminary title report so you know what liens are on the property.

- It's critical to get accurate loan balances along with penalties, late charges, and attorney fees that lenders usually add in.

- Lenders who hold mortgages on the property need to be motivated to work with you. In most cases, if lenders aren't willing to talk to you about discounting their loan(s) to avoid ending up with the property, you're wasting your time.

- Typically, the total cost of acquiring a property needs to be 80 percent or less of the market value to be worthwhile. This is assuming the property is in fairly good condition. Of course, as the home's condition goes down, the discount must go up.

Eleven Things to Consider Before Making an Offer

Whether you're looking for an existing green home or one that you can remodel, here are some important things to keep in mind before you commit:

1. How far are you willing to drive or commute? This will determine the radius of your buying area. If you're considering buying a home to fix up, the closer to where you now live, the better you'll enjoy the process. One couple who bought a home 130 miles away, planning to turn it into their environmentally friendly dream home, spent so much time commuting to their project that they became discouraged; they ended up selling it for a loss.

2. Good schools add value to a neighborhood and should be considered in your purchase decision. Also, if you're interested in a certain school, verify the boundaries with the school district, because they can change yearly.

3. Determine what style of home you are interested in and why. Additionally, look at how the home is situated on the lot. Is it compatible with solar gain or solar roof panels, if those are on your project list? Many buyers become caught up with a home's architecture and charm and then discover after moving in that the home doesn't meet their efficiency needs.

4. What type of floor plan will be most compatible with your lifestyle? If you have trouble climbing stairs, you'll probably want to consider only ranch or single-level homes. Consider room-to-room traffic flow, kitchen work flow, and number of bedrooms and baths as well. Just because a home is green doesn't mean you have to skimp on a home's livability.

5. How close do you need to be to shopping, places of worship, and

recreational facilities? These are important not only to maintaining the value of your home, but enjoying it, too. Being environmentally responsible doesn't mean you have to be dissatisfied with your home or its location.

6. Drive by the home you're interested in at night. Is it a target for headlights? Do cars entering or exiting the street create an annoyance or light up the bedroom?

7. Are there noises in the area at night that you didn't notice during the day? Nearby businesses that you may not have taken note of can be especially busy in the evening. Likewise, early morning noises can create a problem; loading dock, shipyard, and train station noise can carry quite a distance.

8. Make sure the costs of the home plus the improvements you plan to make don't boost the home's price above the neighborhood average. If you're using a contractor, get bids on upgrades before you commit.

9. Visit the home on a weekday. Commuters may use the street in front of the house as a shortcut to the freeway. Neighborhoods that are quiet on weekends may be noisy on weekdays.

10. Is the neighborhood compatible with your lifestyle? Are you looking for a neighborhood with kids in a certain age range? Do you prefer a quiet street, but the neighbor next door has a teenager who likes to rebuild motorcycles on weekends? The best way to find out about a neighborhood is to walk around and talk to several neighbors. If there are problems or negatives, you'll hear about them fast.

11. Get a home inspection so you know whether there are expensive problems lurking in dark places.

Planning an exit strategy is as important as buying. Keep in mind that the best time to think of selling a home is when you buy it.

SHOPPING FOR AN ECO-FRIENDLY HOME ON YOUR OWN

As pointed out earlier in this chapter, working with a green agent or one experienced in eco-friendly homes can make house hunting much easier, especially because the seller normally pays the fees. But if you feel for some reason you don't want work with a buyers' agent or can't find one in your area who is eco-savvy, or you know of a green home you can buy directly from the owner, some sources are:

- The Web site www.ecobroker.com, which has a growing database of green homes for sale across the country. Go to their Web site and click on the homes for sale tab. You will be prompted to key in your location info and any amenities that are important to you.

- Other Web sites you may also want to check out include:

  www.greenhomesforsale.com

  www.greenhomesforsale.com/alllistings.php

  www.listedgreen.com

- Local magazines and newspapers that cater to environmentally conscious readers. These are often good sources for ads featuring green homes for sale. You can even run your own ad as a buyer to express interest in green homes within your price range.

- Buyers' ads, which you can place on Web classified ad sites, such as craigslist.com and similar sites hosted by local radio and television stations.

- Flyers detailing what you're looking for in a home, which should include a little about you and your price range. Compile a list of contacts drawn from architects, builders, landscapers, and others specializing in green homes and send or e-mail them your flyer.

- Or simply drive through an area you're interested in every few days. Look for "For Sale" signs and talk to homeowners.

If you do decide to shop for a home on your own, you'll also you'll need to line up the following professionals:

- A home inspector to evaluate a home you're interested in to make sure it doesn't have serious flaws. Check your local yellow pages under "home inspectors" or go to www.ashi.org to locate an inspector near you who is a member of the American Society of Home Inspectors (ASHI). The Web site to find an Energy Star-approved inspector for your area is: www.energystar.gov/index.cfm?fuseaction=new_homes_partners. showHomesSearch

- Green architects and contractors who specialize in this field. If you're planning on rehabbing a home, they can be important to your project. Check out local eco-friendly publications, suppliers, and builders for referrals.

- As discussed in chapter 1, it's important that you line up your financing up-front so you know what price range to look at. You should also have a loan approval letter from your mortgage lender. If you're using alternative financing or cash, then you'll want other documentation that assures the seller that you can perform.

- A real estate attorney to advise you or close the transaction, or a title company to do the title work or close the transaction, if that's the practice in your state.

Making an Offer on a Home That's For Sale by Owner (FSBO)

Most areas of the country do not yet offer a large inventory of green homes for sale. Often, owners of such homes opt to find buyers on their own through networking, advertising in local publications, and Web sites. If you find an eco-friendly home and want to deal directly with the owner, the following steps show you how to put the deal together:

- Get at least three sets of your state's Offer to Purchase forms and addendums. These are usually available at local stationery and office suppliers. Also, gather Seller Property Disclosure forms and other forms your state may require to complete a home sale. If you are in a state that requires that an attorney close the deal, he or she can furnish you with the approved forms you'll need. Another alternative is to hire an attorney or local real estate agent to do the paperwork for you.

- When they've found a home to make an offer for, most buyers' first concern is what to offer. Many green homes are one of a kind, and chances are that not many similar homes have recently sold in the area to use as market comparisons. The seller's price may be a patch of blue sky or it may be just right. If you feel that the price is fair, based on your experience looking at other homes, then make an offer at or close to the asking sale price. If the price is more than you think the home is worth, make an offer subject to an appraisal.

- When you fill out the purchase forms, be sure to state in the inspection section that the offer is subject to an energy audit and home inspection. If either one reveals problems you don't want to tackle, you can back out of the deal.

- You'll need to include an earnest money deposit with your offer. This can range from a few hundred to several thousand dollars, depending what the sellers agree to. It's a good idea to write in the offer that the closing attorney or title company will hold your earnest money deposit in their trust account.

- Call the owner and make an appointment so you can present your offer. Usually there's some give and take in negotiating the offer, but once an agreement is reached, any changes are written on an addendum and signed by both parties.

- Once the paperwork is completed, copies go to your mortgage lender and to the closing attorney or title/escrow company.

- It's always a good idea to accompany inspectors when they evaluate the property. If problems are discovered, the inspector can tell you how serious they are and offer an estimate of what it will cost to fix them. This is important if you need to go back to the seller and negotiate a repair or price concession.

Mark and Alonzo went the FSBO route when they bought an existing green home near a Utah ski resort. They were seeking an existing energy efficient home built to Energy Star specs with solar panel power generation so they could be independent of the local power company. They figured they could offer up to $950,000.

Going through local brokers, they found nothing in the price range they wanted, so they networked among friends and other green homeowners in the area. After several months, Mark got a tip that a homeowner was talking about selling and moving to a warmer climate. He called the owner and found he was indeed thinking of selling, so Mark set up an appointment to look at the home.

The owner wanted $995,000 for the home; both Mark and Alonzo thought this was on the high side, so they offered to pay for a professional appraisal if the owner would consider selling for the price it was assessed at. Reluctantly the owner agreed to consider an appraisal, but refused to commit to selling for the appraised price. In spite of this, the buyers decided to move ahead and hire an appraiser approved by both parties.

About ten days later, the appraiser e-mailed his appraisal to both buyers and the seller. In his opinion the home was worth $920,000. Understandably, the seller was disappointed. He had spent a lot of money upgrading his home to be energy efficient and installing an expensive solar electrical system.

The seller, upset with the figures, called the appraiser, who explained that improvements and upgrades don't always increase a home's value dollar for dollar. Value is based on what similar homes had sold for, as well as a depreciation factor.

For several weeks the seller stalled, unwilling to move ahead with the sale. It was now the middle of October. An early snowstorm left behind a couple of feet of snow and shut down access to the area for three days, dropping temperatures into the low teens. Although great for skiers, it didn't make the seller too happy, and he decided that Arizona was a much warmer place to live. He called Mark and agreed to sell at the appraised price. A closing in three weeks was agreed upon.

Before the deal could close, a couple of inspections were needed, though. The first, a home inspection, was routine, and a local inspector was hired to complete that. But the second was more complicated; the buyers wanted an inspection of the solar power system. They wanted to be sure the solar panels, inverter, batteries, and wiring were all in good working condition.

The brothers found an electrical contractor with a good reputation who installed solar systems. The contractor agreed for a reasonable fee ($350) to inspect the system. He found a malfunctioning panel that he estimated would cost about $1,200 to repair.

A home inspector's report revealed only a few minor problems and normal home wear and tear, so the buyers decided to ignore those, but did ask the seller to repair or credit them $1,200 to fix the solar panel.

Because these buyers didn't finance the home through a mortgage company or need energy saving credits to qualify, a HERS report was not done. However, the buyers wisely hired a home inspector and an electrical contractor to inspect the solar power equipment. Because home inspectors are not usually trained to inspect specialty equipment or systems, you may need to find a professional to do those.

The important lesson learned is not to hesitate to hire professionals to inspect green homes that have specialized components that other homes don't. It can save you thousands of dollars later on.

There are many traps to buying a green new or existing home. The next chapter shows how to navigate those alligator-infested waters without being bitten.

CHAPTER 3

BUYING A GREEN HOME

This chapter could also be titled *The Art of the Deal,* because it's job is to help you avoid the pitfalls that cost many buyers money, the deal, or both. Shopping for an existing green home or one you can fix up to be energy efficient can be frustrating, and what to offer for one is often difficult to determine, even for the pros.

In this chapter, you'll learn not only how to tame the challenges to making a successful deal, but also how to avoid those toothy alligators that lurk just under the surface...the ones that lunge when least expected and cost you money.

Of course, no home-buying discussion would be complete without covering opportunities inherent in bank-owned properties and working with a lender to avoid foreclosure on a property you're interested in buying.

It all boils down to making offers, and putting deals together is exciting, adrenalin-pumping stuff. In this chapter you'll learn:

- How to find green homes for sale
- How to determine how much to offer for a home

- How low an offer you can make without insulting the seller
- How to get the sellers to pay for closing costs, upgrades, and repairs
- How to protect yourself from unexpected problems
- What to look for in home warranties
- How to take advantage of bank REOs and short sales

LEARNING ABOUT ECO-FRIENDLY HOMES

Whether you're a first timer or a veteran home buyer, the best way to learn about green home values and upgrades is to look at homes—especially homes that have the environmental features you're interested in. Some ways to find homes that are already green are:

- Find tours of green homes sponsored by local green building suppliers, architects, university architect departments, Realtors, and home owners. For example, in Utah a local newspaper once ran an article on a homeowner who installed a solar power system. The owner installed the system because the local utility wanted thousands of dollars more than the homeowner thought was fair to run a line to his new home. On the weekend the article appeared, the owner held an open house so that interested people could drop by, see his solar install, and learn more about solar power generation.

- Look for environmentally focused local magazines, newspapers, and club bulletins that feature homeowners who have completed green projects. Usually these homeowners are proud of their upgrades and welcome inquires and opportunities to show off their projects.

- Network with real estate agents who list and sell green homes. Review their new listings and ask agents if they will allow you to contact previous clients who have bought green homes. Most homeowners who buy green homes are proud of what they're doing and are eager to share their knowledge and ideas with someone who wants to follow in their footsteps.

- Find out who the local green builders are and visit their project sites. This is a great way to get ideas and see how various green building components and systems work.

- Check out magazines such as *Fine Homebuilding, This Old House,*

Natural Home, and other publications that feature cutting-edge green building projects.

If you do your homework, it won't be too long before you start to become an expert on what different green homes and green upgrades cost and what value they add to homes in your area.

SUCCESSFUL STRATEGIES FOR MAKING AN OFFER ON A HOME

As you look at existing green homes or homes that you can upgrade, two big questions should be uppermost in your thinking:

1. What is the home worth? This often boils down to what a buyer is willing to pay and a seller willing to accept.

2. And what can I get it for? Sometimes the only way you can find out is make an offer. No one knows the pressures, motivations, and hidden circumstances that sellers experience when they have your offer in hand.

Sometimes it's not so simple to determine what a home is worth or what you should offer for it, because no two homes are exactly alike, especially green homes. Commonly, appraisers rely on past sales of similar properties to establish a value. If there aren't many comparables, as is usually the case with newer green homes or older ones that have been upgraded, determining fair market value can be challenging. Therefore, it's important to find an appraiser who has a track record of appraising eco-friendly homes.

On the other hand, if you're looking for a home that you can upgrade, determining a home's value is more straightforward; it's like buying any other non-green house in a neighborhood.

Most experienced real estate agents agree that a home is worth what someone is willing to pay. A home may have been expertly appraised at $200,000, but if the colors, the way it sits on the lot, or its floor plan don't appeal to buyers, it can languish on the market and sell, in the end, for $185,000 or less.

Many sellers don't understand this. They receive an inflated drive-by appraisal from a lender for a home equity line of credit and then lock in a price in their mind. After months of being buffeted by the market and rejected by dozens of buyers, they get a clue that perhaps their home is overpriced.

On the flip side, a home may appraise for $185,000. If the colors flow, the decorating is superb, there are few homes like it for sale in the area, and five buyers are making offers, the selling price could easily reach $200,000 or more.

In short, as a buyer, be continually aware that cost is not the same as value. Ignoring this can come back to bite you if you buy a home and then find out you can't do the improvements you want, or you decide to sell and the home won't appraise for what you want.

Suppose you installed a $20,000 photovoltaics system, spent $10,000 in landscaping changes to conserve water, and another $50,000 to remodel the interior of your home. If other homes in the neighborhood don't have these improvements, you've created an over-improved home for the area. This means you may have spent $80,000 in upgrades that won't increase the value of your home by nearly the same amount unless all the owners in the area upgrade their homes as you've done. Even though other environmentally concerned buyers may be impressed by what you've done, they aren't likely to pay you more than the home is worth or what it will appraise for.

Yes, it's unfair that your neighbors' homes determine what your home is worth, but that's life in the fast lane. Bluntly put: if you want to over-improve in a neighborhood, plan on living there a long time, because your enjoyment of the upgrades is likely to be your return on investment. Some homeowners find that acceptable and are happy with it.

The bottom line is that you need to be careful in choosing an area to build or create your green home, because eventually you're going to want, or need, to sell it.

If the high cost of a solar power system is not practical for you, you may be able to buy sustainable power from your local utility. It might cost a little more per kilowatt hour, but it's a lot cheaper than a solar power system, and you'll be reducing your carbon footprint about the same. Check out your local utility to see if this option is available in your area.

Deciding What to Offer on a Home

Once you find a home that's a strong possibility for purchase, consider these pre-offer steps:

• Ask your agent to create a list of similar homes that have sold in the area over the past sixty days. Notice the difference between the average list prices and sales prices. In a normal market, the difference is commonly in the 2 to 5 percent range. A hot sellers' market can easily generate over 100 percent, which indicates that homeowners are getting more than their asking prices and probably dealing with multiple offers. However, a strong buyers' market might generate between 2 and 20 percent, or more, in discounts off asking prices, and how many days a home has been on the market *(DOM)* can easily stretch between six months and a year.

• Look closely at average DOMs, keeping this caution in mind: Some agents will remove a listing from the MLS after a month or two and re-list it so that it appears as a new listing with a low DOM (which is kind of like turning back the odometer on a used car). Ask your agent to check the expired listings function on the MLS to see if this has happened. Also, a home that's been on the market for two or three months doesn't necessarily mean it's been sitting there with no action. There may have been offers that didn't work out or a sale that failed, resulting in the home being put back on the market. Ask sellers if they've had any deals fall apart; often they'll tell you all about it. If the reasons are inspection-related, tread cautiously.

• Other information, such as why the sellers are selling, is also important and can help you fine-tune your offer. A transfer, job loss, or other pressure situation, as well as the home's condition, are important factors to consider.

Neal and Collette used these strategies when they bought a home to fulfill their dream of rehabbing a property into one that's both energy efficient and remodeled with sustainable materials. In putting together a preliminary list from the MLS, their agent picked homes in target neighborhoods priced between $250,000 and $275,000, their pre-approved loan limit.

Going down the list with their agent, Neal and Collette were able to quickly eliminate sixteen homes out of the thirty-seven they started out with. Crossed off the list were homes on busy streets and those recently remodeled or with styles the buyers didn't like. They would need to inspect the remaining twenty-one homes personally.

Because they wanted to install a solar water heating system, it was important that the roof slope face south, which eliminated another eight homes on the list. The ninth home was a possibility, as were three others. But a vacant home clicked. It had good southern exposure, it hadn't been remodeled, and the location was excellent. It was exactly what they were looking for and priced at $254,900. Hurrying through the last four homes confirmed their choice: the 1970s ranch on a cul-de-sac was the one they wanted to make an offer on.

Once you make a decision on a home, it's important to put together an offer fast. It's a competitive world, and other buyers may have the same taste as yours. Seasoned agents can tell of many instances when homes sat on the market for weeks with no activity, and then suddenly several offers came in the same day.

To help Neal and Colette decide what price to offer, the buyers' agent, Andrea, looked at what other similar homes had sold for in the area the last thirty days. She noticed that the average listing sold for 96 percent of list price; days-on-market averaged sixty-seven, and this particular home had been on the market for seventy-four days.

Andrea called the listing agent (who was new and talkative) and found out that the owners had moved to another state due to a job change. This meant that pressure was on the sellers to get their home sold. This was good news for the prospective buyers, as it could soften the price a little.

Neal and Collette decided to offer $239,600, about 6 percent less than the asking price of $254,900, which they felt was in line with market conditions. As it turned out they were lucky and no competing offers surfaced. The pre-approval letter (see Chapter 1) convinced the sellers it was a bird-in-the-hand they shouldn't pass up, especially because the home sat vacant, eating up over $1,230 a month in interest and taxes.

Handling an Overpriced Home

To some homeowners, their house becomes an extension of their egos. They overprice their home, reasoning that if the Adam's home down the street sold for $280,000, then theirs must be worth at least $295,000. How long it takes owners who overprice their homes to wake up to the reality of their situation depends on how much pressure there is for them to sell.

This is especially true when owners have installed energy efficient and green upgrades and feel they should reap a dollar-for-dollar return. In many areas, there are not a lot of homes with green upgrades for sale, so it's hard to find similar sold properties to use as comparables to establish value. As

a result, these sellers put unrealistic prices on their properties and the properties languish on the market, becoming white elephants that local agents
are reluctant to show.

In one case, an owner built an energy efficient earth-covered home with
solar water heating panels for domestic hot water to heat an indoor swimming pool. It was an eco-friendly marvel built, where possible, with sustainable materials. Unfortunately, after a couple of years the owners had to
sell, and they put the home on the market for $1.5 million. It quickly
became apparent that this was not going to be a fast sale. Curb appeal was
atrocious. From the street, the home looked like a small hill covered with
weeds that were fast crowding out the wild flowers the owner had planted.

Although the home may have easily cost the million and a half to build,
it was in a neighborhood with homes in the $300,000 to $400,000 range.
Five years later, the home is still on the market, and just about every real
estate agency in town has watched one of their "For Sale" signs rust on the
property. As the technology and hardware age on this overbuilt home, it will
become even less attractive to a green buyer. Will it ever sell? A few dozen
brokers are wondering and watching.

In many cases, you'll find it's more attractive and cost effective to
upgrade an existing home with cutting edge technology rather than buy a
home upgraded a few years ago. Green technology (like your cell phone) is
improving so rapidly that after a few years hardware can depreciate like a
laptop with 512K RAM and a 20MB hard drive.

If a home is overpriced and the owner is unrealistic as to its worth,
it's sometimes better to walk away and find another property. However, if
you feel the situation is worth pursuing, there are a number of strategies you
can try:

• Keep an eye on the house in the hope that the price will come down
to what you think it's worth. This, of course, has its hazards; it might sell
before the price drops to what you are willing to pay.

• Make an offer for what you think the house is worth. If the sellers
reject your offer or counter with a price you think is still too high, you're
no worse off than you were before you made the offer.

• Offer to pay what a professional appraiser appraises the home for.
With this approach, a neutral third party ends up setting the price. This
offers the sellers a way out without having to admit that they may have

priced the home too high and gives an out-of-area owner who doesn't know local values a reality check.

Of course, it helps if you talk to a couple of appraisers first and find out approximately what the home will appraise for, so that you can get your financial ducks in a row.

At the same time, you might ignore or be uninformed about market values and lose the home you want. This can happen when friends or relatives tell you they can remember when that house sold for $150,000 years ago and insist that they wouldn't pay a dime over $170,000 for it today. It's best to ignore this kind of hot air and trust the advice of real estate professionals who know the market.

Making It Easy for the Seller to Accept Your Offer

When you inspect a listing that interests you, listen closely when the sellers talk about their plans, problems, or concerns in selling the home or moving. The more of these concerns you can solve for them in your offer, the better. Many times little concessions on your part won't cost you anything, but will make a deal doable.

For example, if the sellers need to close in three weeks or less and you can speed up your financing, you've strengthened your offer. On the flip side, the sellers may be sixty days from their new home being finished. You can do a delayed closing or a thirty-day (or whatever works) rent back after closing, where the seller pays rent equal to your monthly payment.

The key is to make your offer as difficult as possible for the sellers to counter. Sometimes the terms, timing, or moving schedule is more important than the offer price. You or your agent can chat with the owners or their listing agent and find out what their hot buttons are. It's amazing how many listing agents and sellers have loose lips; they can't stop talking! You just have to smile, listen, and take notes.

Here are some tips to help you with your negotiations:

• Establish rapport with the sellers by finding common ground. If the home is an existing green home, you'll have a lot in common. Also look for common hobbies, colleges or schools attended, kids' ages, environmental concerns, etc.

• Never bad-mouth the home to the sellers or their agent. If there are problems, address them specifically in an offer or addendum after the inspection. Remember, sellers have an attachment to their home; ego is involved. When you point out flaws, you create bad feelings and throw up obstacles to your offer. This doesn't get you a better deal.

• Understand that the sellers are often emotionally involved in their home. If, for instance, they've buried a beloved pet in the back yard, tell them you'll maintain the site and respect it. If they're into birds, let them know you'll continue to keep their feeders filled. You get the idea.

Protecting Yourself When You Make an Offer

The goal is to put a deal together, get your offer accepted, and move smoothly to closing. However, life throws us unexpected curves and unforeseen things happen to the best of plans. So, it's important to plan for this in your offers by putting addendums and clauses in your offers. Here are some steps you can take to protect yourself when you make your offer:

• Make sure your offer is subject to your qualifying for the loan. Even though you're approved by the bank, you still need this protection. In one case, a buyer didn't write in a subject-to-loan-approval clause because he didn't want to weaken his offer. Unfortunately, a few days before closing, he lost his job when his company had to lay people off because they lost a major contract. As a result, the buyer couldn't close, and he lost his $2,500 deposit.

• Include an addendum with a list of all items the sellers agree to include in the sale. Also, take digital photos of the items and create a print in album format (four to six images per page) and attach it to the paperwork. Every experienced agent has horror stories of sellers taking items when moving out that they shouldn't have. Most common are appliances, light fixtures and chandeliers, air conditioners, ceiling fans, and window coverings. If you have an addendum that the sellers must sign with photos of the items, they are less likely to get loaded on the movers truck.

• Take care that you get copies of all documents, including the addendums numbered 1/x, 2/x, etc. Getting a complete set of documents up front is the only way you can protect yourself from problems that can arise later on from missing or altered documents.

• Any agreements you make with the sellers, such as early closing, extended closing, or other agreements, should be in writing on an addendum. Chisel in concrete: If it's not in writing, it doesn't exist.

• Make your offer subject to home, HERS, and specialized equipment inspections. These inspections may cost you a few hundred dollars more, but can save you from making costly mistakes such as a broken solar panel or burnt out inverter.

• Insist that your agent presents the offer in person. If the property is vacant and the sellers are not in the area, a conference call between the sellers and both agents will work. You absolutely don't want your offer faxed to the listing agent. He or she can shop the offer by calling other buyers and agents who have shown the house trying to get a better deal. Also, insist that the offer expires upon presentation. You don't want your offer sitting on the sellers' kitchen table for a day or so motivating other buyers to write a little better deal.

• If you're offering less than the maximum loan that you qualify for on your pre-approval letter, ask that the lender rewrite the letter for the offer amount. When you're making a low offer for $235,000, you don't want the sellers to know that you qualify for $250,000. In one instance, an inexperienced agent cost his clients several thousand dollars when he presented an offer on a home at $7,500 under the asking price of $242,500. The listing agent asked to see the buyer's pre-qualification letter and immediately noticed the amount they qualified for was $250,000. The sellers, under pressure to sell, would have taken the low offer, but when they saw the buyers qualified for much more, they countered for $5,000 more and got it.

GETTING THE SELLER TO PAY CONCESSIONS

There are many ways that sellers can tack on inducements to lure buyers. They can offer appliances, vacations, cars, cash-backs, and so on. But the concessions you are most likely to find important to making a deal are those that help you buy the home, correct problems, or give you peace of mind. Three common situations you'll likely encounter are:

1. The sellers offer to pay some or all of your closing costs as an inducement to buy their property.

2. The sellers may offer to give you a painting, carpeting, or other allowance as an incentive.

3. If you've made an offer subject to an inspection and the inspector has found problems, you go back to the seller with a written request to fix the problems or cancel the deal.

🏠 Typical Seller Concessions

Item	What you get
Points and buy downs	Each point equals 1 percent of the loan amount. Depending on the market, 2 points can buy down your interest rate about a quarter of a percent. This can help you qualify to buy their house.
Closing costs	FHA/VA and other loan programs allow the sellers to pay for many buyer closing costs. Your lender can work up the amount you'll need to ask for in the offer.
Paint, carpet, or other upgrades	In a slow market, this is a good way to upgrade the house a notch or two without money out of your pocket. Get bids so that you can ask for a specific amount.
Seller rent back	If they can't move out immediately, the sellers can rent back for the amount of your payment. Typically, divide the monthly payment by thirty to figure the daily rent. This can be a good way to go when you have a lease with a month or two left and you need to close to receive a good interest rate.
Appliances that normally wouldn't go with the house.	Especially in a slow market, you can often get the sellers to leave a refrigerator or other appliances you need by including them in the offer.

Item	What you get
Carpet and/or house cleaning	It doesn't hurt to add in the offer that the sellers will have the house and carpets professionally cleaned when they move out. This will make your move-in much nicer.
Home warranties and inspections	If the sellers haven't already included a home warranty, write it in. You may get away with adding home inspections too.

Getting the Seller to Pay All or Part of Your Closing Costs

When you ask the sellers to pay all or part of the closing costs or other concessions to help you buy the house, you may have to go full price or over to make it work. The sellers may not have enough equity or may be unwilling to agree to the full amount you've requested.

For example, if a home is priced at $257,000 and you want the sellers to pay $6,500 of your closing costs as a concession, you may have to add all or part of the cost to the sales price. If you had to add all the closing costs to the purchase price, the price would increase to $265,500 in the worst-case scenario. Keep in mind that you have to be careful not to add too much to the sales price, or the house may not appraise for the higher amount. In one particular case, after the appraisal was completed, the buyers came up short and needed to increase the price by $3,000 to cover closing costs. The lender called the appraiser and asked her if she could fine-tune her appraisal, increasing it to meet the increased price. The appraiser looked at the comparable sales she used in the appraisal and the HERS report and agreed to the increase.

Sometimes with an energy efficient mortgage, the upgrades you're planning on adding can kick up the appraisal enough to cover some or all of the closing costs.

A common response to asking the sellers to pay all the closing costs is a counter-offer to split the difference. In the above example, this would mean increasing the home price by $3,250, with the sellers paying the other $3,250.

However, if the sellers have no *equity* in their home (their loan balance equals the sales price), they have no room to maneuver because the home is already priced so they walk away with zero. You then have to decide whether the house is worth increasing your price to cover concessions and whether over time it will appraise for the increased amount. In these cases, you need to rely on your agent's experience and neighborhood home values to guide you.

In the end, determining what to ask for in concessions is more art form than particle physics. Sellers often don't know what's acceptable until a signed offer stares up at them from the table. Sometimes they take offers they should counter, and other times they reject offers they should grab. It all comes down to the ebb and flow of the sellers' states of mind and what's happening in their lives at the time.

In one case, sellers rejected an offer that required them to pay $7,500 toward the buyer's closing costs; the next day the sellers found out that an offer they had made on a home in another state had been accepted. That changed everything. Money suddenly took a back seat to getting out of town as fast as possible. The sellers called their agent back, told him they had changed their minds, and asked if he could retrieve the offer. They were now willing to sign!

Seller Allowances

Occasionally you'll find sellers who offer buyers an allowance to replace appliances, carpet, or other items they don't want to deal with fixing or replacing. For instance, an ad or listing could state that there's a $4,500 carpet allowance or $3,000 painting allowance and so on.

One seller, who was too lazy to fix up his home, offered $10,000 cash back at closing because the kitchen cabinets had a bad paint job and the appliances were old. Not surprisingly, the home languished on the market for months until the owner, who had already moved, could no longer make the payments and the bank started foreclosure. Seller allowances should raise a red flag, because it's likely the owners have let maintenance problems slide and usually don't have the money to correct them.

If you consider making an offer on a home with seller allowances, get material and labor bids on the costs to make the house comparable to others in its price range. Compare the bids to the seller allowance. It's likely you'll still need to subtract a few thousand dollars more from the listed price to make it a workable deal.

Concessions Due to Inspection Problems

It's a good idea to make offers subject to professional inspections. If an inspector finds problems that you don't want to tackle, you can cancel the deal and get your deposit back.

Suppose the inspector of a house you've made an offer on finds half a dozen problems, from a cracked combustion chamber in an older furnace to spliced wiring outside a junction box: about $2,500 worth of replacements and fix-ups. You can consider one of these options:

- Send a notice to the listing agent and sellers that you want to cancel the transaction.

- Offer to move forward with the deal if the sellers replace the furnace and take care of the other problems listed in the inspection report.

- Negotiate with the sellers, offering to take care of some of the problems if they take care of others.

- If the sellers refuse to make any concessions and if you want the property badly enough, you'll have to buy it as it is. While this was common in the days of hot sellers' markets, with depreciating house prices in much of the country, it's no longer the norm. Sellers who take this stance are likely to see a rusting frame and peeling paint on their "For Sale" sign.

If the home you're interested in has special energy efficient hardware such as boilers, solar collectors, electrical systems, etc., as part of your inspection, you'll want to make sure any warranties are transferable. You may also want to make sure that parts and service are easily available from a local company. You want to avoid scenarios like having a roof-mounted solar water heating system and no access to parts or service if it breaks down, ensuring that you'll end up with an expensive roof ornament.

Appraisals and Repairs

When an appraiser goes through a home during a conventional loan appraisal, he is primary concerned with value. Any obvious problems, of course, will be flagged as a loan condition and need to be repaired.

FHA/VA appraisals are more thorough and detailed in their inspection.

The appraiser may poke around in the attic, climb down in the crawl space, and check windows for cracks or failed seals. As for the roof, it must have least three years' life left before it needs replacing. Appraisers not only look at value, but want to make sure that the buyer won't have to make any repairs for at least a year. However, FHA/VA appraisals are not professional home inspections, nor are the appraisers trained to be inspectors.

If you've made an offer on a home and the appraisal comes back with a list of repairs, the sellers really don't have any alternative if the sale is to move forward other than to make the repairs. Sometimes under extenuating circumstances, such as bad weather that prevents roof work or exterior painting or repairs, a lender may allow money to be escrowed for a short time so the loan can close. But buying a home "as is," as often happened in the old days, is no longer an option. Not when there are lenders, appraisals, and inspections involved.

Combining Grants and Seller Concessions

Seller concessions when coupled with government energy-efficient grants, tax credits, and rebates can make buying a home even easier. Local utility companies also have attractive offers and discounts for upgrading insulation and appliances.

Although many agents are aware of these programs, frequent changes are the norm, so it's important for you to be proactive and do some homework to find out what's currently available in our area. For example, one Utah community pays up to $4,000 to help first time home buyers buy in targeted areas. If the buyers live in the home for five years, the down payment loan is forgiven. Add $300 rebates for upgrading to energy saving appliances, rebates for upgrading insulation and Energy Star programs, and buyers can be helped out significantly.

FILLING OUT PURCHASE AGREEMENT PAPERWORK

Every state has its own real estate purchase agreements that require you to fill in the blanks. If you're working with an agent, he or she will handle all the paperwork. If you don't have an agent, consult an attorney to ensure the paperwork is filled out correctly and you're protected. It's easy to get into a dispute with a seller over an earnest money deposit should the deal flounder along the way.

To find a home inspector, check the Yellow Pages or look for Web sites, or consult the following:

American Society of Home Inspectors
932 Lee St., Ste. 101
Des Plaines, IL 60016
Tel. (800) 290-2744
www.ashi.com

National Association of Property Inspectors
303 W. Cypress St.
San Antonio, TX 78212
Tel. (800) 486-3676 or (210) 225-2897
http://napi.lincoln-grad.org

National Association of Certified Home Inspectors
PO Box 987
Valley Forge, PA 19482
www.nachi.org

National Association of Home Inspectors
4248 Park Glen Rd.
Minneapolis, MN 55416
Tel. (800) 448-3942 or (612) 928-4641
www.nahi.org

Be sure to talk to three inspectors, get references, and make sure a return visit to confirm repairs is included in the fee.

BUYING A HOME WARRANTY CAN SAVE YOU MONEY

Buying a home does carry some risk. Since you haven't lived in the home and the sellers may not necessarily be forthcoming about what they know, you don't know what works and what problems lurk in hidden places.

To minimize this risk, you can buy a one-year insurance policy for between $300 and $500 that covers electrical, heating, and plumbing systems. Also covered are built-in appliances such as dishwashers, disposals, compactors, and range/ovens. Refrigerators, air conditioners, washers, and dryers are not usually included in the basic coverage of most policies, but they can be covered for an additional fee.

Also important are riders that warrant other hardware not normally covered, such as solar panels, pumps, boilers, inverters, and heating systems. You may have to talk to several insurers to find one that will include extra coverage for these items. In any case, read the fine print of any policy for exclusions.

How Home Warranties Work

Typically, if you're covered by home warranty programs and have a repair problem, you call the warranty company, which sends a repair person from its own local network of contractors. Since the contractor usually charges a service charge of $35 to $50 for each call, it pays to handle the small or inexpensive repairs yourself.

The major benefit of a warranty is protection from problems you didn't notice during the inspection. But it's important to realize that most warranties don't cover structural repairs such as a roof or foundation. There are, though, a growing number of companies that do offer, for a higher premium, coverage for structural and roofing work. Also, coverage of plumbing systems varies widely. Some policies cover all pipes, inside the home and out, but others don't. You'll need to read the fine print to find out what's covered and not covered.

One of the most important policy restrictions to look for is "pre-existing conditions." Many warranty programs don't cover problems that may have been present and detectable before the policy went into effect. The coverage varies widely, so it's important to read and compare policies carefully before buying.

Regulation of home warranties varies from state to state. In some states, the real estate commission is the regulator, but in others the department of insurance has jurisdiction. In reality, the only way to find out what you're getting is to read the policy over carefully and verify the company's financial stability.

What to Look for in a Home Warranty

Different regions of the country require different emphasis on what is covered. In the Sunbelt, for instance, air-conditioning and pool coverage are important, but in the Northeast furnaces and sprinkling systems would be primary concerns. Regardless of the area in which you live, in choosing a policy:

• Make sure the insurer is financially sound and has a good track record. The best policy is worthless if the company goes bankrupt. Look for companies tied in with substantial national corporations that usually advertise in your local Yellow Pages. Check with a real estate broker or two for companies they have had good experiences with. It doesn't hurt to verify customer references or check financial filings at the department of real estate or insurance either.

• Read the policy through and make sure you understand what is and is not covered, as well as what the company charges for the service fee. On the average, most service fees run in the $35 to $50 range. But remember, it's a matter of trade-offs, and the lowest service fee is not always the best deal.

• Look carefully at the "pre-existing conditions" part of the policy. Does the insurer require a presale home inspection before the policy becomes effective, and is there a time period before certain items are covered after you move in?

• Make sure the optional coverage you want, such as swimming pool, air conditioning, or refrigerator, is included. If a seller is furnishing only a bare bones policy, you may need to pay the extra cost for the options you want. It's a good idea to read over the policy before closing. When you're moving in and the air conditioner dies on the hottest day of the year is a bad time to find out the seller gave you only a basic policy.

• Make sure, if the home has energy efficient hardware you want covered, that a rider specifying the additional inclusions is in your hand before closing.

Appraisals are not inspections. Many buyers believe that an appraisal will uncover problems in a home. While it's true that obvious problems will be flagged, appraisers are not home inspectors. An appraiser's job is to make sure the property's market value is in line with the sales price, to protect the bank's investment.

TAKING ADVANTAGE OF BANK REOs AND SHORT SALES

It's amazing how many home buyers who want an existing home start out by asking about foreclosures and *REOs* (Real Estate Owned: homes that lenders have foreclosed on and now own). Foreclosures, REOs, and the lesser known *short sales* (covered later in the Short Sales section) all create opportunities to cash in on distressed properties.

Since foreclosures were covered in chapter 2, the next sections will focus on the pros and cons of REOs and of working with lenders to discount the loan balance when a property owner is in trouble and can't make payments (hence the term short sale).

Buying REOs

It costs in the neighborhood of $20,000 to $30,000 in attorney's fees, administration costs, and carrying costs for a bank to foreclose on a property. If the home is damaged and needs work to make it saleable, the costs go up dramatically.

Typically, when you make a low offer on an REO, the bank will look at the costs they've incurred on this particular home. They'll also consider the chances of getting a better deal in the near future. If the market is slow and they've had this home on the books for awhile, the chances are good you'll get a deal. In other words, the right timing helps.

But there are also caveats. If the home needs work, you'll need to tread carefully. Many times, buyers acquire such homes and find out that the costs of restoration can equal or exceed the savings they hoped to get on their good deal.

The first step in buying an REO is go through the home carefully and make a list of needed repairs and estimated costs. Then add the costs to the price you're willing to pay for the home and compare with what similar homes have sold for in the area. The total should be 15 to 20 percent less than what comparable homes have sold for in the area. If you go to the trouble of jumping through the REO committee's paperwork hoops, it should be worth your while. Hopefully, the REO committee will be in a good mood that day and accept your offer.

Occasionally, you'll stumble across an REO in a neighborhood you're interested in and want to make an offer. In one case, home buyers Shawn and Marie found an REO in a neighborhood they liked that was close to an elementary school their daughter went to. In going through the house, they found it was in bad shape. The lawn was dead, the carpets beyond cleaning, the appliances needed to be replaced, and five doors had holes in them.

The first thing Shawn and Marie did was to invest $650 in two inspections: $300 for a professional home inspection and $350 for a HERS inspection. They knew spending the money was a gamble, but they needed to know exactly what it would cost to upgrade the house to a livable and energy efficient condition. After they had gotten the inspection reports back, they shopped around for carpets, Energy Star appliances, insulation, and windows. They also gathered contractor bids for work they couldn't do themselves. Their total costs would be $33,578, including their inspection reports.

The buyers then asked their agent to check on the MLS for what other similar properties had sold for the last thirty days. According to the print-out, $285,000 appeared to be the current market value. Similar homes currently for sale in the area confirmed that price range.

Shawn felt that if they were going to all that trouble fixing up the home and dealing with the REO people, they should get a good deal. Putting a sharp pencil to the figures, they decided to offer the bank $220,000 for the home. Their agent wrote up the offer and attached a copy of the bids and repair list they had put together, along with the inspection reports and the buyer's mortgage pre-approval letter. The package was overnighted to the bank's REO representative who was handling the case. About five days later, Shawn and Marie's agent got a call from the REO department that they had accepted the offer. After subtracting fix-up costs, the buyers had essentially gotten a home for about $31,000 under market value in a desirable area. Not a bad return on the work they would need to do to make it their dream home.

The key to getting a bank REO committee to look at an offer is to include supporting data such as bids, cost lists, inspections, comparable sales, and a pre-approval letter that shows the buyers are ready to go. Lenders are influenced by bird-in-the-hand offers, just like homeowners.

Short Sales

In a slow market, a home can drop in value to less than the owner's mortgage balance. In mortgage speak, this is called *upside down* or *negative equity*. If a homeowner has to sell in this situation, it can get ugly fast because there are few good options.

One way to deal with this scenario is a short sale. Essentially, a *short sale* is when the bank agrees to take less than owed on the mortgage to avoid the costs of foreclosing. To get this option underway, the homeowner needs to contact the bank's customer service department to see if they'll deal.

Usually the bank will send the homeowner a questionnaire to fill out and return. If the bank believes the situation warrants a short sale, they'll agree to look at offers.

Your first step as a possible buyer is to write a purchase offer and include a pre-approval letter from your lender along with the same paperwork you would put together for an REO bid. This collection is submitted to the bank's representative assigned to the case. It's likely several people will be involved in the decision process, so it's hard to predict how long it will take for the bank to get back to you with an acceptance, counter, or rejection. Typically, it ranges from a few days to a couple of weeks.

Whether the sellers' bank accepts the offer depends on the market, how many payments the seller is behind, and whether your deal is less than the costs of a foreclosure.

The bottom line is that you can often get a good deal with a short sale, but you usually need a lot of time and patience. Sometimes the sellers are cooperative because they want to save their credit. At other times they give up part way through, and the deal fizzles because the bank can't deal directly with you as long the sellers continue to own the property.

In spite of their drawbacks, short sales can be a good option if you run across a seller with upside down equity who needs to sell.

Admittedly, green house hunting and the hassles of upgrading an existing home to create an eco-friendly home is not for everyone. If building a new home quickens your pulse and fires the imagination, then you'll find the next chapter exciting. It explains how to find and work with green contractors to create the energy efficient and sustainable home of your dreams.

Quick Guide to Writing an Offer

Question	Answer
What should we offer?	Have your agent look up what similar homes have sold for in the area in the last few months. Check out the list price/sold price ratio and the days-on-market of these sales. Find out if the sellers are under pressure to sell. Look at what concessions sellers are paying in your area.
How low can we go and not lose the house?	If the average home is selling for 3 percent under list, that's a good place to start. If it's a competitive market, offers much lower than this can cost you the house. If it's a slow market, consider another 5 percent reduction in price or concessions.
How about concessions? (Seller paid points, buy downs, and closing costs)	It's often more difficult to get the sellers to pay both concessions and a price cut. If you need seller concessions to put the deal together, these will take priority over the price. You may even have to up the price slightly.
What other inducements can we offer so the seller will accept our offer.	Sometimes timing is more important than money. Maybe a sixty-day close or a close and rent back to the sellers for a few months will solve a problem. Find out what the sellers' problems are and propose a win-win solution.
What if the sellers are asking too much and won't come down?	If your offer is fair for the market and the home's condition, show them comparable homes that have sold the last couple of months. If that doesn't work, write up an offer where a certified appraiser sets the price. Put in writing that the sellers pay the appraiser if they back out. Otherwise, you pay it.

 PART 2

BUILDING AN ECO-FRIENDLY HOME

CHAPTER 4

FINDING AND WORKING WITH A GREEN BUILDER

If the thought of redoing someone else's decorating and landscaping doesn't float your boat, new construction may be the way to go. Many home buyers find owning a one-of-a-kind property—and that new house smell and fresh look—hard to resist. There's also a lot to be said for the fun of starting from scratch and designing an energy efficient home exactly the way you want it. It's not only exciting to incorporate the latest technology and use environmentally friendly materials in your design, but you can create a much healthier home to live in.

To help you navigate the rapids of planning and building an environmentally friendly home, the following pages give you an overview of how to find and work with green architects, builders, tradesmen, and others in the building process. To help you make your new green home building experience a success, in this chapter you'll learn:

- What constitutes a green home
- What to do to plan your environmentally friendly home
- How to find and work with a green architect

- How to find and work with a green builder
- How to protect yourself with good paperwork
- How to buy a green home in a new subdivision
- What you should check out before committing to build a green home

WHAT CONSTITUTES A GREEN HOME?

Although several national green home certification programs, as well as many local guidelines, are gaining momentum, they all essentially accomplish the same broad goals, specifying that a green home:

- Be at least 15 percent more energy efficient than standard construction
- Waste fewer resources during construction and site prep
- Use sustainable materials where possible
- Recycle water and materials
- Create a more healthful and comfortable environment
- Reduce the home's carbon footprint

How well builders achieve these goals in new home construction depends on climate, location, political will, and especially consumers who demand that new homes conform to green standards. Builders build what homebuyers want to buy. If buyers demand homes that are energy efficient and use sustainable materials, building practices throughout the country will soon change for the greener.

Minimum Green Building Standards

In addition to many local and regional green building programs, a federal agency and two national organizations have established their own minimum green building standards. You'll be hearing a lot more about these three rating systems over the next few years, as builders embrace certification programs to increase sales. The big three are:

1. *The National Association of Home Builders (NAHB)* is a national non-profit organization that has developed a set of green guidelines for its members. Because its members build nearly 80 percent of the country's new homes each year, their system will have a big impact.

2. *The U.S. Green Building Council* is another national non-profit organization that has rolled out a three-level residential certification program through the Leadership in Energy and Environmental Design programs (LEED).

3. *Energy Star and Water Sense* are the federal government's green programs, and they require homes to be at least 15 percent more efficient than homes built to the 2004 residential code. Energy Star programs have been around for a few years, and many building products and appliances now qualify to display their logo and energy guide stickers.

Along with architects and builders who embrace their standards, the NAHB, LEED, and federal Energy Star and Water Sense programs are resources that can make creating and building your dream eco-friendly home much easier than ever before. The key to a hassle-free project is to do the necessary homework so you can communicate your dream to the architect and/or builder so they can design your home to these green standards.

 Web sites worth checking out are:

www. nahb.org—National Homebuilders Association (NAHB)

www. usgbc.org—The U.S. Green Building Council developed the Leadership in Energy and Environmental Design (LEED) programs for certifying green homes.

www.energystar.gov.homes—Web site for the federal government's Energy Star and Water Sense programs.

Confusion in Green Building Standards

It's important to point out that there are many differences of opinion and trade-offs regarding what contributes to a green home. And those trade-offs often differ depending on climate, location, labor availability, and other costs. Unfortunately, they can also present a moving target as technology improves and product sources and building techniques change. But that's the thrill of being on the cutting edge of becoming carbon neutral.

Some building products may be advertised as green because they come from sustainable materials. But the energy expended shipping these materials to a building site might more than offset the gain. Perhaps the manufacturing process produces hazardous by-products, excess waste that adds to landfills, and other environmental problems. It's important to read the fine print and consider the big picture before embracing a product just because it sports a green label.

In one case, a homeowner in the Northwest proudly showed off his bamboo flooring while telling his guests how it saved trees. One guest pointed out that while trees in Washington State are abundant and wood flooring is produced locally, bamboo, on the other hand, is transported from thousands of miles away. Shipping consumes energy and is a big source of carbon pollution. Is there a real benefit here?

Obviously there are serious trade-offs to consider before blindly following the latest fads. Picking and choosing materials for a new home can be both challenging and fun, but you'll have to take a hands-on approach and seek out sustainable materials that make sense for your area. Your builder or designer may or may not be as environmentally sensitive as you are in incorporating local sustainable materials into your building plans.

In other words, building green takes more than just telling a builder you want a green home. Your builder's vision of an environmentally responsible home may not be the same as yours.

PLANNING YOUR ENVIRONMENTALLY FRIENDLY HOME

In addition to using green products, good design is the other major factor involved in planning an environmentally friendly home. Designing a home to take advantage of solar gain, thermal mass, and cross ventilation are just a few fundamentals that need to be considered up-front. The home should be designed from the ground up to be as energy efficient and carbon neutral as possible.

Tacking on a few energy saving products and appliances to an existing home design usually doesn't cut it. Many builders are taking these shortcuts and advertising their homes as green to lure in buyers. (This is sometimes referred to as *green-washing*.) It's important to remember that quality and energy efficiency vary greatly among builders, so in the homebuilding marketplace, it's still buyer beware.

One criticism of the government's Energy Star program is that it requires builders to exceed the 2004 code by only 15 percent, which is not very hard to do. Putting in Energy Star-rated appliances, windows, and extra insulation easily allows the builder to advertise the home as green. Yes, every bit helps, but the technology and products that are currently available far exceed 15 percent. It's even possible now to build more than 100 percent more efficiently than the older code.

If you're serious about building a new home as eco-friendly as possible, it all boils down to the fact you'll need to do some serious homework and get a few ducks lined up. This is especially important before you shop for an architect or builder.

Does It Cost More to Build Green?

There's no fast and hard answer to whether it actually costs more to build green. It depends on the area, materials, and design, plus your goals. How much work can you do on the home and what will you have to sub-contract? Many homeowners find that they can cut costs significantly by using recycled materials and adding sweat equity.

Although some building experts say it costs about 15 percent more to build a home green as opposed to regular construction, they also acknowledge that the extra costs usually pay for themselves in a few years. After the breakeven point, the energy savings more than make the initial investment worthwhile.

In reality, you won't be able to accurately pinpoint your construction costs until you go over your plans with an architect or builder and crunch some numbers. If you're like most homeowners, you'll start out with bigger-than-you-can-afford plans and then scale them down to the real world.

Common variables that most impact a green home's cost are:

- Where you build your home. In most areas, the farther away from core business districts you go, the less land costs. If you have to commute, it's important to factor that in. Spending two hours daily in your car commuting to a green home becomes a trade-off that doesn't help your goal of becoming carbon-neutral.

- Site fees, such as running utilities (gas, power, sewer, and water), hookup fees, local impact fees, building permit costs, inspection fees, and so on.

- Local climate. Obviously, a home in Minnesota will require a different insulation and design package than one in Florida.

- The style and square footage of your home.

- The amenities you want, such as appliances, fireplaces, heating systems, etc.

- Federal, state, and local tax credits and rebates for installing energy efficient products.

- The current cost of utilities in your area.

Adding some energy efficient components later on and spreading the costs over several years is a way many homeowners achieve their dream of a green home. For example, one couple plumbed their home so they could add a solar hot water system later on. Another homeowner wired his home so he could convert to solar power in the future.

It's extremely important to decide up-front what kind of home you want: the floor plan, amenities, landscaping, and so on. If it takes a year or two of homework to crystallize your thinking, so be it. You don't want to make changes after construction starts. Additions and change orders are a builder's profit center and your budget buster.

How Much Money Do You Have to Work With?

The most important factor in planning to build a green home is how much money you have to spend. If you haven't talked to a lender yet, you may want to review Chapter 1 and get a pre-approval letter (Figure 1-1). If you're building a new home, then the approval would be for a construction loan that would convert to permanent financing when the home is completed.

It's also important to factor in about 15 percent of the home's total cost for unanticipated costs, such a material cost increases, changes, and upgrades. Once you have determined the maximum amount your mortgage lender will loan you, subtract about 15 percent to keep in reserve. For example, if you qualify for a $589,000 loan, subtracting $88,350, or 15 percent, leaves $500,650 for your targeted home price.

Of course, if you get into the construction phase and see that the project is progressing as bid, you can always find places to spend the reserve. Many homeowners who build new homes find that after they move in they wish they had budgeted more money for landscaping or other overlooked items.

Even if you are buying a home in a new subdivision and the costs are known, you'll still need a reserve for items the builder doesn't cover. You won't enjoy your new home as much if you max out your credit cards and mortgage loan limit to complete an overbudget home.

Why Use an Architect?

Even though it typically adds 10 to 15 percent to your green home project to work with an architect, it's worth it. Here are several reasons why:

• Building an energy efficient home out of sustainable materials is more complex than buying an off-the-shelf-type build job in a typical subdivision. Professional help can save you costly mistakes.

• An architect can guide you in selecting green materials and building methods to help you achieve your goals. Because the green building field is growing rapidly, professionals who are current on the latest green products and technology can often save you more than they cost.

• If you haven't crystallized your thinking about what you want, an architect can work with you on a green design that will fit both your budget and lifestyle.

• Hopefully you're going to be living in the home for a long time, and it's probably going to be your biggest investment. You want to make sure it's built to LEED standards and local codes and that all the components work together toward a carbon-zero home.

• One of the biggest pluses in using a green architect is that he or she will likely have a working relationship with like-minded contractors, subcontractors, and suppliers. This alone can make the difference between ending up with a dream home or an unfinished, overbudget nightmare.

• You're spending a lot of money on a dream home, and the design and components must work together in harmony or you won't be happy living in it. It's amazing how many people who build new homes sell after a couple of years because they don't feel comfortable living in them. After a few months they find out the floor plan doesn't fit their lifestyle or the home is too big or too small. There's a better and cheaper way to do it, and that's to take the time to get it right the first time around.

• All homes are eventually sold, and well designed floor plans and quality construction increase the value more and make them easier to sell than lesser quality homes. Yes, a home is a place to live, but it's also an important investment that someday you'll want to cash in.

For example, a homeowner bought a $12,000 solar hot water system from a company that marketed their system through high pressure sales tactics (the kind where you get a free dinner). For the first eighteen months the system worked as promised, but when a problem developed with one of the solar collectors, the owner found out the company had gone out of business. There was no one locally who handled solar collectors, and it took several months before the owner was able to track down someone who could replace it. After a lot of time, frustration, and spending a couple of thousand dollars, the homeowner finally got the system back on line.

Had this homeowner been working with a knowledgeable architect or contractor, it's unlikely she would have ended up with the problems she did. Professionals usually work with reliable venders with good track records who back up their warranties.

FINDING AND WORKING WITH A GREEN ARCHITECT

If you're like most people who dream of building a home that uses sustainable materials and is energy efficient, you've probably collected dozens of clipped articles, photos, product sources, and so on. You may have also sketched out floor plans and jotted down how you want the home to flow. This is all good. The more you've gelled your thinking about what's important to you in a home, the easier it will be to turn that dream into reality.

After you've completed the loan paperwork and have that loan approval letter in hand, the serious work of finding an architect bubbles to the top. This step of the process is critical. You may have to interview several before finding an architect that fires your imagination and creates a synergy that results in a one-of-kind home plan.

Finding a Green Architect

So how do you find a green architect who can translate your dream into a home? Some suggestions are:

- Start by asking other homeowners whose homes you admire who did their design.

- Talk with builders who specialize in green homes about who they use and can recommend.

- Read local publications that target environmental issues, because they often have advertisements or articles written by design professionals.

- Ask suppliers of eco-friendly products for recommendations.

- Check out the architectural department of a local university for referrals.

You'll want to put together a list of several architects to interview. The goal is to find one who not only has technical skills and a track record but is compatible with you. And most importantly, one who is willing to listen to what you want and will try to turn your dream into a reality.

Questions to Ask During Your Interviews

Don't be discouraged if have to interview several architects before you find one you're comfortable with. But before you commit, consider the following questions:

- Does the firm have a track record in green construction?

- Can the firm give you the names of several past clients for you to speak with? If you can, ask referrals if you can drop by and see their homes. Most green homeowners are delighted to show off what they've accomplished and their approaches to saving energy; you may have a hard time leaving.

- Does the architect listen to what you want and work to design it, or does she try to push her ideas?

- Do your personalities mesh? If not, move on to the next architect on your list no matter how appealing that person's track record. Working with a professional on the design of your dream home is going to be an intensely emotional project. There's no room for egos and agendas to muddy the process. Ideally, the designer and the client create a synergy that often results in a home the owners are thrilled with.

Don't be discouraged if you find out you have champagne tastes and a beer budget; it's normal. That's why you hired a professional. She or he can help you cut costs, learn where you can add sweat equity, find used materials, and/or defer some items until later when you have better cash flow.

Probably one of the most important resources architects bring to the table is their contacts. They know who the best green builders are, and that gives you a head start on finding the next important professional on your project.

FINDING AND WORKING WITH A GREEN BUILDER

One of the most critical steps in building your energy efficient home is making sure everyone involved is on the same page. If you, the architect, the builder, and others are not sharing the same vision of what you want to accomplish, the end results are going to make you a frustrated and unhappy homeowner.

Most problems between home buyers and builders come from poor communication and not following sound paperwork procedures. And because green building terms, standards, and materials are new and subject to whomever is doing the job, it's easy to end up with results that are not what you envisioned and costs that balloon way over budget.

You want to avoid builders who don't have a clue as to how various components of energy efficiency and the environment fit together holistically. Some builders try to jump on the green bandwagon by adding a few Energy Star-rated appliances, windows, and insulation so they can certify their homes as green construction.

For instance, one builder of a small twenty-seven-lot subdivision advertised his project as green and environmentally sensitive. Yet driving through the project, you could see that many homes were built with southside garages, while others with full southern exposures had only a few small windows. Solar panels for power or hot water were nonexistent, and landscaping was left up to the buyer, without water capture or storage system options. As for putting in low water-using plants and trees, owners were on their own.

The builder in this case had installed highly energy efficient furnaces, windows, and appliances and offered a few environmentally friendly floor covering options, but otherwise it was business (building) as usual. Obviously he was attempting to attract well-meaning but uninformed buyers with the "go green" flyers and ads that featured his homes as earth-friendly and responsible.

This is a common problem for consumers looking to make their lives more earth-friendly by buying or building a green home. The developers and builders' ads and claims are confusing and muddy the water considerably. But if you've done your homework, you'll be able to easily spot—and avoid—green-washing.

Finding a Green Builder

Similar to finding a Realtor, architect, or lender, you need to do some homework, put together a list of potential green builders, and then narrow it down. Yes, it's tedious and a pain, but the stakes are so high that you don't want to shortcut the process. Possible sources for referrals for green builders include:

- Your architect or others on the design side. These are usually high quality options for the top of your list.

- Contractors or subcontractors. They may be able to recommend others in their industry who specialize in green construction.

- Suppliers of green products. They often know who the best builders are.

- Realtors who sell green homes. They can often refer you to builders who have good reputations.

Once you've put together a list of green builders, the goal is to narrow it down to the top three that you will interview and ask to submit a bid based on your plans and specs. Follow a similar approach to the one you used in deciding on an architect. Make sure you both share the same vision of your dream home and can work together.

Before you interview the builders on your shortlist, check with your state's contractor licensing agency and make sure that person is currently licensed and insured. You can find that out by going to www.contractorslicense.org and clicking on your state. Here's what to keep in mind:

- Verify that prospects are a general contractor or have the building specialty license they claim to have. You don't want someone who isn't experienced or licensed doing the type of work you want done. Some apprentices may claim to be masters or journeymen, when they're not.

- Work only with licensed contractors and subcontractors. They want to protect their licenses and are less likely to skip out on a job or do shoddy work.

- Make sure the contractor is bonded and insured. That guarantees that if one of their employees is injured on the job, you won't be facing a hefty bill or lawsuit.

- Check with the Better Business Bureau or your state's consumer protection agency to see if any complaints have been filed. Several complaints should eliminate that contractor from consideration.

Only after you've ensured that the contractors on your short list have passed the above tests should you take the next step and set up appointments to meet with builders and go over your plans for a bid. At least, that's the theory. In real life, finding good contractors isn't always easy. For instance:

- There may not be that many quality green builders in your area to choose from

- The builder you really want is backlogged and can't get to you until 2015

- Another builder on your short list won't even return your e-mails or phone calls

- There's no builder in your area who specializes or is interested in doing green homes

- A builder everyone says does great work was just convicted of fraud

And so on. Regardless of how many builders you end up interviewing, one or several, there are a few questions you'll want to ask upfront.

Questions to Ask During Your Interviews

Don't hesitate to ask about anything you don't understand, especially terms and builder jargon. Remember, the only stupid question is the one you didn't ask. Some information you want to get up front follows:

- Ask how many years they have owned the business. Contractors have a high failure rate the first several years, and it's a good sign if they have survived and prospered more than five years.

- Ask for a copy of their construction contract. Well-written and professional paperwork is a big plus. However, you may still want to have a real estate attorney look it over.

- Ask for details of their insurance coverage. You want to see proof of workers' compensation coverage, liability, and umbrella policies.

Get a list of the past five to ten jobs, along with the homeowners' names, addresses, phone numbers, or e-mail addresses. You'll want to talk to several past clients to see if their experiences with this builder were positive. Don't hesitate to call a contractor's past clients. Most people are flattered when fellow green homebuilders seek out their opinion. It's likely these people will invite you to see their home. Wouldn't you like to show off your home's energy-saving features to someone who takes the environment seriously?

Deciding on Which Bid to Accept

You may think that choosing among competing bids is going to be like calculating a moon-shot trajectory, but in reality they are seldom grouped that closely. Here are some tips that'll help you through the process:

•   Low bids are not likely to be top quality or the best choice. Perhaps the estimator missed something, or maybe the builder will ask for more money to complete the project. Be suspicious of any bids that are substantially lower than the others.

•   On the other end of the spectrum, the highest bid isn't a guarantee of good work or necessarily the best choice. Some builders submit high bids when they don't want the job; it's a good way to say no without offending anyone.

•   Most often bids in the middle are more realistic—the ones you should focus on. It then becomes a matter of picking the builder with whom you feel most comfortable and who has the best track record.

What if You Can't Find a Green Builder in Your Area?

Since builders with solid track records of building green homes are still rare in some areas, you may have to work with one who doesn't passionately share your vision of a green world. But that's okay, it can still work out. Be a little more careful in the selection process and discuss your goals in depth with the builder. It's important for you and the builder to have good rapport and to be able to communicate. If the builder is a skilled professional and you're working with an architect, the three of you should be able to build your green dream home without too many problems.

Most home building problems happen because:

- All agreements are not specifically and clearly put in writing.

- Homeowners shortcut their homework and hire a builder who doesn't have a good track record, is financially shaky, or lacks the skills to build a first-rate project.

- The architect, builder, or homeowner don't get along or are not communicating.

- The homeowner wants to make major changes along the way.

- All parties are not on the same page on work flow, payment, and time schedules.

- Homeowner and builder are not communicating on a daily basis. They should have a brief what-we're-doing-today meeting first thing each morning.

- The homeowner insists on making changes that add to the cost and create an over-budget problem. You should resist the temptation to say to the builder, *"While you're at it, could you...?"* These are words that lead to many cost over-runs. Resist adding items and change orders as if they were from the dark side.

- There's not complete agreement in writing detailing the scope of any homeowner sweat equity that's factored in as part of the total cost.

If you're building your green home without using an architect, you'll need to make sure your builder has necessary experience and skills and is willing to learn to work with new materials and installation techniques.

Typically, the contractor hires subcontractors to install various components, such as electrical, plumbing, framing, exterior sheathing, insulation, roofing, and so on. You'll need to stay on top of the construction and make sure you're getting what you pay for—and want. You may also seriously consider hiring a professional building inspector or engineer to keep tabs on the construction.

PROTECTING YOURSELF WITH GOOD PAPERWORK

Putting everything in writing is so critical that you should chisel on a stone tablet:

If it isn't in writing, it doesn't exist.

This means all extensions, change orders, new agreements, product changes, deadlines, and so on should be in writing on addendums, signed by all parties, dated, and numbered 1 of X. A contract that clearly spells everything out will eliminate most of the communication problems that can arise during construction.

An effective contract should at least include:

- Project starting and ending dates.

- A clear understanding as to who gets the building permits and pays the fees. Usually the builder takes out the permits and you reimburse the fees, or they may be part of the bid.

- Information as to who supervises the subcontractors, handles problems, and is the boots-on-the-project to make sure everyone is on the same page.

- How the contractor plans on protecting the home from construction dust and debris. It should be specific, such as using 6-ml plastic sheeting or tarps supported by framework enclosing the work area.

- Change orders, which are especially important. What happens if you see something that looked great on paper but doesn't look as good as the project takes shape? Right: it's written up on a change order form or addendum that breaks down material costs and labor.

- All warranties or guarantees, which should be specific as to what they do and don't cover and for how long they are valid.

- A provision in your agreement for binding arbitration in the event there are disputes.

- Work and material, which should be specific and broken down as to product model numbers, amounts, costs, sizes, and so on.

- Any sweat equity, which should be broken down specifically as to what you will do and when, and the dollar amount you are credited.

- Copies of the contractor's insurance coverage certificates. These should include workers' compensation, personal liability, and property damage policies.

Of course, you also want to read through the paperwork and make sure you understand everything clearly. It's also a good idea to have an attorney check the contract out.

⌂ Two good Web sites on contracts are:

www.b4ubuild.com/resources/contract/index.shtml

www.askthebuilder.com/B318_15_Helpful_Clauses_for_Construction_
Contracts.shtml

Paying the Contractor and Managing Your Costs

Typically, a builder will ask for a deposit up-front, which should not exceed 10 percent of the contract amount. As the construction progresses, you and/or the construction lender release funds as certain benchmarks, such as foundation completion, framing, sheathing, etc., are completed. What these benchmarks are and how much money is released should be clearly spelled out in the contract.

Change orders are usually paid for by check or credit card (never cash) at the time they are ordered. For example, suppose you didn't include a solar power generating system you really wanted but couldn't afford. Then suddenly your Aunt Sadie dies and leaves you $25,000. You tell the builder you now want to add the solar power system. He works out the details and tells you it will be $18,975 installed. You agree, and the builder writes up a change order that everyone signs and you pay the bill.

Of course, the change order copy and credit card receipt or check copy should be stapled to the paperwork. Never pay with cash because it's important to create an unbroken paper trail with matching payment receipts in case there's a dispute later on.

Adding Sweat Equity to Your Project

Depending on your availability and skills, you can save money by doing some of the work yourself. The contractor probably won't agree to allow you to do code work, such as electrical, plumbing, roofing, or framing. His license is on the line, and if you screw up it can cause him serious problems. However, grunt work may be a good way to save a few bucks.

Introduce the idea of sweat equity during the bid negotiating phase. It may be a good idea to have the builder work up two bids: one with sweat equity work included and the other without.

One builder who receives many requests from clients who want to earn sweat equity reports that when clients look at the bids and see how much time and commitment is needed, most end up backing out. Still, if you have skills in the building trades, you can save some bucks.

Another option that you may want to consider in your quest for an energy efficient home is to start within an existing subdivision where the builder is building green homes. True, it's not as fun as building your custom dream home, but then not everyone can afford, or wants to drive, BMWs either.

Shopping for a Green Home in a New Subdivision

If you can't afford a new custom-built green home and rehabbing an existing home to be eco-friendly doesn't excite you, then you may want to consider a new home in a green subdivision.

Step one, of course, is to find out what your friendly mortgage lender will commit to loaning you. With your lender's pre-approval letter in hand, you're ready to go shopping.

Step two is to make a list of green communities in areas you're interested in. Before you waste a lot of time driving out to see them, call to find out the median price of the homes. Many builders have Web sites where you can check out the models, energy-saving options, and pricing.

Don't go by the starting price in a builder's advertising. Builders rarely offer or sell homes at the bottom of their price range. It's similar to buying a car. You may be attracted to a dealer by the low advertised price, but when you get there you find it's a stripped down model. The salesperson then pressures you to upgrade. New home builders are masters at this. By the time you get through the options and upgrades, the real price range starts about halfway up the scale. If you plan on this from the beginning, you'll save a lot of running around. This is not to say that builders are dishonest, just that new home marketing stretches the envelope a little to attract people. This is especially true when the term *green* can be interpreted many different ways.

EIGHT THINGS YOU SHOULD CHECK OUT BEFORE YOU COMMIT

When you find your dream home, the pressure is on to sign the paperwork and move on to the fun stuff. However, that can cause you problems later on. Before you ink the paperwork, take a deep breath and check out the following:

1.   Builders often try to pressure you to use their lender. They want to minimize the chance for deals to fall through, and controlling the financing is one way to do this. They may offer upgrades or interest buy downs if you choose their financing. The best way to find out if these incentives are really deals is get a good faith estimate from the builder's lender (see chapter 1). Compare it with estimates from a couple of other lenders, and the best deal will become obvious. If you do find a better deal than the builder is offering and opt not to use their financing, your mortgage pre-approval letter should satisfy most builders that you're a genuine, qualified buyer.

2.   Get copies of the *CC & R (Covenants, Conditions & Restrictions)* and *HOA (Homeowner's Association)* rules. Read them over carefully, because these documents will tell you what you can and can't do with your property. For example, you might be prohibited from parking an RV next to your home. Landscaping restrictions may apply. One home buyer had a motor home that he wanted to park on an extended driveway next to his home. Unfortunately, he didn't read the CC & Rs before he bought. When he started to work on a driveway extension, he found out quickly that RVs were not allowed on the home sites. This ended up costing him $35 a month at an RV storage lot about a mile away.

3.   Research the builder. Check with the Better Business Bureau and a state contractor's board if you have one. Research not only the company but also the builder, through his or her personal name. You want to know if complaints have been filed and how many, and whether the builder has gone bankrupt recently. If lots of complaints about the company or builder surface, seriously consider shopping elsewhere.

4.   Walk around the community and talk to at least three new home owners. Ask them how they like the builder and how promptly problems or complaints were handled. Especially important is how many items were on their punch list (a list of problems discovered on the final walk through before closing) and how long it took the builder to take care of them. If the *punch list* is more than a dozen items and repair is slow, you'll want to find out why.

5.   Ask the sales person or builder rep how close to the completion

date homes are finished. If possible, get a copy of the construction schedule. A builder whose projections are behind a month or two may cause you problems if you have to be out of a home or rental on a certain date. This is another red flag to consider.

6. If you find a model you absolutely love and want to put a deal together, make sure you get everything you want in writing. Remember the chiseled-in-stone saying at the beginning of the chapter, painfully learned and relearned: *If it isn't in writing, it doesn't exist.* Verbal promises are nothing more than hot air; you can't enforce anything not in writing.

7. Get a price list for the options and upgrades. Don't ever sign any paperwork unless you know exactly what an item costs. To be filled in later is an absolute no no. Also, never leave the sales office without copies of all the paperwork. Too many buyers run into problems later because they didn't get copies of addendums covering upgrades and options.

Ben and Wendy found this out the hard way when they bought a home in the first phase of a new green community. The salesman told them the massive rock fireplace with a pellet insert (a $6,500 option) was included in the model they picked out, and they took his word for it. Several weeks later, when they did a framing walk-through, they noticed the concrete and framing for a fireplace were missing. As it turned out, a fireplace for that model was not standard and the salesperson who wrote up the sales contract no longer worked for the builder. You guessed it—there was nothing in the paperwork about a fireplace. Ben and Wendy had to write a check for half the option, or $3,250, to add it, with the balance due in thirty days. Obviously they weren't happy about it, but there was nothing they could do without losing a sizeable deposit if they backed out. It can't be stressed too strongly: Get it in writing. Make sure you receive copies of all documents and number the addendums 1/x, 2/x, etc. Missing addendums usually cause the most problems because that's where changes and contract modifications are written.

8. Make sure you understand the paragraphs in the purchase contract that specify when you close. Builders often pressure you to close before the house is finished or items on the punch list are completed. Don't close before all items on the list are done. Deal with this up front and get it in writing on an addendum if you have to.

Before you buy a new home, recommended reads are:

The Ultimate New-Home Buying Guide, by Jeff and Susan Treganowan (Maple Leaf Press, 2001)

Your New House: The Alert Consumers Guide to Buying and Building a Quality Home, by Alan Fields and Denise Fields (Windsor Peak Press, 2002)

"Buying a new home: How to read the fine print of contracts." (Executive Living: Special Advertising Supplement): *San Diego Business Journal* (Digital - Jul 28, 2005), available from Amazon.com

This chapter has covered a lot of ground about finding and working with professionals who can help you buy or build your dream green home. Chapter 5 gives you an overview of the various energy efficient products and sustainable materials that you can choose from to build your dream home.

CHAPTER 5

PLANNING YOUR NEW GREEN HOME

After you've decided on an architect and builder or have found a great subdivision that has models built to NAHB, LEED, or Energy Star specifications, the next challenge is deciding what green components you want in your new home.

News about the latest in eco-friendly technology and green products appears practically daily. Newspapers, magazines, radio shows, and television shows—especially home improvement programs—regularly tout the most recent information regarding environmental responsibility. Incorporating all these new technologies and energy saving advances all at once can be overwhelming and certainly unrealistic, even if it were possible. Reducing energy dependence and improving the environment is both an attitude and a long-term process. You might say planning is an opportunity to practice your personal *Kaizen,* a Japanese management strategy that roughly translates into continuous, slow improvement by working smarter.

If you're like most homebuyers, in addition to how much your friendly banker will lend, you'll also have to work within the realities of a down payment. And that likely means you'll have to make trade-offs. You'll have to choose which energy-saving products you will be able to incorporate into your plans now and which you will have to defer until later.

Sometimes it takes a lot of creativity to accomplish the most with the resources you have to work with. The creativity and innovations that homeowners bring to their projects are amazing. Many owners are proud of what they have accomplished with a limited budget and are eager to share their wisdom.

To help you plan your project while keeping an eye on your budget, this chapter gives you an overview of some of the different green components available.

In this chapter you'll learn:

- What some of the available passive energy saving options are

- How to get fresh air into an airtight house

- How to determine whether solar or wind power is for you

- How the use of sustainable products leads to reduced costs

- How to avoid the seven biggest mistakes many new green homeowners make

Utilizing Passive Energy Saving Options

After decades of ignoring our environment and building homes wherever, however, and whatever size we wanted, no matter how energy inefficient and wasteful, it's beginning to dawn on us that our natural resources may be finite. As energy costs spiral upwards, building techniques used by the ancient Greeks and early American colonists are starting to look more attractive. These early craftsmen worked hard to find ways to use the environment to their advantage. They didn't have a choice. If they ignored their environment, they froze in winter and sweltered in summer.

Although for most of us, conservation is not yet that drastic, some people have realized that it's critical to conserve what we have, and they're dragging the rest of us kicking and screaming to the same conclusion. As the green movement grows and becomes increasingly mainstream, "rediscovered" energy-saving techniques can help reduce greenhouse gases. As an added bonus, we may also discover a renewed sense of harmony with our homes and environment.

During the design stage of building your new eco-friendly home, an oldie but goodie energy-saving step is to work with your architect to ensure that your home will be positioned on the lot to take advantage of passive heating and cooling physics. This entails:

- Positioning the house for maximum solar gain
- Creating a floor plan in which your garage and utility areas are opposite south-facing living areas
- Designing the home for efficient air flow
- Installing energy efficient windows for maximum solar gain
- Using green heating and cooling technologies
- Installing a high efficiency insulation package geared to your climate

Positioning Your Home for Southern Exposure

A passive solar house designed to take maximum advantage of solar gain has large amounts of glass on its southeast, south, and southwest sides. For example, a 1,700-square foot home may have 600 square feet or more of southern exposure glass, with few or no windows on the north-facing walls. In cold winter areas, you'll want to keep the square footage allocated to doors and windows in north-facing walls to about 10 percent or less.

True north and magnetic north are not the same. The magnetic north you read with a compass changes slightly each year, while true north stays the same. The difference in degrees between true north and compass north is declination and can vary up to 20 degrees, depending on where you live. To find true north, go to www.ngdc.noaa.gov/seg/geomag/jsp/Declination.jsp and key in your zip code, then click on the "Compute Declination" button. If the reading is XX degrees xx minutes East (Western U.S.), subtract this figure from your compass reading to get true north. Conversely, if the declination reading is XX degrees xx minutes West (Eastern U.S.), add that reading to your magnetic north compass to get true north.

For example, if you were boating in Long Island Sound and set the compass needle to magnetic north, you would add 14 degrees to locate true north (i.e., rotate your compass 14 degrees clockwise). In Utah, where the declination is about 14 degrees east, you would rotate the needle counter-clockwise. The zero point where magnetic and true north are the same is on a meandering vertical line running slightly west of the Great Lakes from Canada to the Gulf of Mexico.

The key to maximizing solar gain is to orient the home so the long-side axis runs east-west, with the living side facing true south. In winter, the low-angle sun will provide heat; in summer, a roof overhang will prevent the high-angle sunlight from causing excessive heat buildup.

How far a roof overhang extends from the wall depends on window sizes and geographic location. This is something your architect should be able to calculate for your location.

Sometimes you don't have much control over your home's orientation. In an established subdivision, picking a south-facing lot would be your first choice. But that's not always possible, especially if most of the lots are already sold. South-facing lots are usually the first to sell.

All is not lost. Sometimes you can get such a great deal on a nonsouth-facing lot that the savings can help you add a sun room or solarium to capture solar heat. A good architect or savvy green builder can design a house plan that fits the lot and overcomes its limitations.

Creating an Energy Efficient Floor Plan

Design the home to take advantage of as many environmental factors as possible, including southern exposure. Some of the most common strategies include:

- Positioning the garage, storage rooms, and laundry room at the rear of a south-facing home. This gives the living areas, family room, kitchen, and as many bedrooms as possible the benefits of solar gain in winter.

- Designing the house so that the southeast to southwest arc has as much glass area as possible to maximize solar gain.

- Including massive rock fireplaces, concrete walls, tile floors, and even water-filled containers to absorb solar heat during the day. In the evening, these structures release stored heat to moderate indoor temperature swings.

- Designing with a high ratio of interior space to exterior size. This strategy uses less energy to heat or cool. In cold winter regions, the design should be more of a square than a rectangle. For example, the long side should be no more than 1.3 times the home's short side. If the west- or east-facing short side is 30 feet, then the long side would be no longer than 39 feet for a 1,170-square-foot floor plan.

- Adding a second story about the same size could yield a 2,300-square-foot moderate-sized Salt Box home, popular in New England and other cold weather areas. Lengthen the house's long side to 1.6 to 2.5 times the short side in climates where winters are not so severe. Further south, where the climate becomes hot and humid, lengthening the long-side ratio 1.7 to 3.0 makes cross ventilation more efficient. Shortening the ratio to 1.3 to 1.6 times the short side maximizes the interior space in relation to the exterior wall surface area. In the Southwest, this reduces heat gain in the hot, arid climate. Steeply pitched roofs to handle heavy snow loads are no longer needed, so flat roofs become the norm.

- Planting deciduous trees, which shade in the summer when leafed out but allow good solar gain during late fall and winter when leaves have fallen.

Designing for Efficient Air Distribution

When buying a lot in an established subdivision, you probably won't have much leeway on where your home is sited. Setbacks, utility lines, easements, and other regulations usually dictate where and how the house is built. In these cases, the key to building the most energy efficient design is to choose a development early enough so you can pick out a lot that fits your plan. The early bird gets the best lots, and southern-facing lots usually sell first. If you have a lot or piece of land big enough to allow more options, you can take advantage of your site's micro-climate to further reduce energy costs. Based on the conditions, consider the following:

- In hot climates, it's important to design and position your home so it takes advantage of cooling airflow. For passive cooling to work, there must be a constant flow of cooler air through the home. Screened porches, windows, fans, and efficient vents, along with good insulation, keep air conditioning use to a minimum.

- On a sloping lot, it's often more energy efficient to build the house to take advantage of airflow. For example, in a hot Southern climate, building close to the ridge top would capture cool breezes. In desert climates, cool air collects in valleys, so you would want to build further down the slope. Building about halfway up the slope may be the best strategy for a temperate location.

- Airflow and micro-climates are affected by trees, land forms, lakes, streams, and other factors. You'll need to determine how wind directions affect your building site at different times of the day. Commonly, cold air breezes travel downhill in the mornings and reverse as the valley heats up and warm air rises.

- In cold winter locations, you can use evergreen trees, buildings, and land forms to protect the home from winter winds. Warmer locations can also use similar buffers to channel cooling air into the home.

- Building within natural drainages or depressions can put the home in the path of cold air as it flows downhill. You can build earthen berms or other structures to divert airflow, but these can increase your site costs dramatically. It can be more economical to keep shopping for a better building site.

By now you can see that there are not only many environmental factors to consider, but that the home's design should closely fit the location and climate to create a truly energy efficient home.

In addition to carefully choosing the site and design, the materials you use to build the home are vital to the equation. Shopping around and doing some homework will help you decide on which products are the most energy efficient and will give you the best return on your investment

Installing Energy Efficient Windows

When designing your home, windows are one area where you don't want to cut corners. They are critical not only to the enjoyment you get from living in the home, but to its energy efficiency. This doesn't mean that you necessarily have to buy and install top national brands. Many local window makers make excellent products that are equally as good as the heavily advertised brands. And when you buy local, you can usually save on shipping costs and their contribution to greenhouse gases.

Your architect or builder will specify the type and size of the windows in the plans and may also recommend certain brands. Even though the recommended brands are likely quality windows, you'll still want to do some comparison shopping since you're the one both writing the checks and living in the house. Keep in mind that window manufacturing is a competitive industry; frequent product and technology changes can become confusing. But there are shopping tools that will help you compare and get the best product for the best price.

Start by looking for an Energy Star sticker. This tells you it meets minimum government standards for energy efficiency. It doesn't, however, tell which window is best suited for your project or if it's the best price. Look for a *National Fenestration Rating Council (NFRC)* sticker. The NFRC provides third-party performance ratings for windows and doors that allow you to compare products on an equal footing.

For example, suppose you are looking for a 4-foot by 5-foot double pane, gas-filled window. The supplier may show you several national brands priced from $489 to $550 and a local brand priced at $445. Normally it would be difficult to determine which window is the best deal. Likely, you would have to rely on a brand name that may or may not be the best product for the money. But if the windows sport NFRC stickers, you can make a more informed decision. Here's what an NFRC sticks tells you:

• The top of the sticker describes the window type. For instance, it could be vinyl-clad aluminum sash, double-glazed, argon-filled, horizontal slider, low E. Argon gas is a better insulator than air, and the optimal gap between glass panes is one-half inch. Low E glass coatings reflect solar heat; this is great in Arizona, but maybe not so good in Alaska. Double glazing (two panes) is standard, but triple glazing gives better performance in cold climates. Some coastal areas require impact-resistant glass as well.

• The sticker's next section, *Energy Performance Ratings*, covers U-Factor (US/I-P) and the Solar Heat Gain Coefficient. The U-Factor is the opposite of R-Value; the lower the number, the better the rating. This factor is the sum of all the windows' components expressed as a number. The lower the number (.30 or lower), the more energy efficient the window. The other rating, *Solar Heat Gain Coefficient*, is the percentage of solar heat that gets into the house. A low heat gain number, like 0.35, is good for hot climates, while higher ratings of 0.50 through 0.70+ are more effective in Minnesota winters, where you want all the solar gain you can get.

• The next section on the sticker is *Additional Performance Ratings*, with two rating numbers, *Visible Transmittance* and *Air Leakage*. These numbers are additional ratings that may be required by local codes. A lower number reflects better performance.

• A useful rating is *Condensation Resistance*. This number (0 through 100) predicts the likelihood that the window will fog up with condensation. A higher number equals less potential condensation. This rating is handy for comparing different types of windows: slider versus double-hung, for instance.

After you determine the best price/ratings combination, the next equally important item you need to compare is the warranty. Because windows are expensive high-performance products, you should insist on a good warranty. If all else is equal, but window A is slightly more expensive and has a better warranty than window B, it's usually best to go with A, based on the warranty.

There are five things to keep in mind when reviewing window warranties:

1. A good warranty guarantees the seals for twenty years and the frame and hardware for ten years.

2. Be wary of prorated warranties. Read the fine print; a lot of exclusions should raise a red flag.

3. Be wary of lifetime warranties as well. If a company has only been around for a few years, you have no guarantee it'll be there five years from now, let alone for a lifetime.

4. If it's a local company, how long have they been in business? Check out their track record: complaints, reputation, and likelihood of being around ten years from now.

5. Beware of warranties that are nontransferable or void if you sell the home. It shouldn't matter who owns the home.

Using Green Heating and Cooling Technology

Some impressive advances in solar heating and cooling technology have evolved in the past few years. Not only have rooftop solar collectors become more efficient, but gone are the ugly canoe-sized units of the 1970s and 1980s. Now solar panels for both heating and power generation look like tiles or black panels that create a low profile on the roof.

Better yet, federal, state, and some local governments and utilities offer tax credits, rebates, or incentives to encourage you to add these energy-saving technologies to your new or existing home. With energy costs spiraling, governments and utilities offering incentives, and renewable energy the rage, it's a perfect storm for green homeowners.

This makes solar water heating a great place to start, especially if your water heater consumes a big chunk of your utility dollars. There are two basic types of solar water heaters, passive and active.

Passive systems have few moving parts. Water circulates from the solar collector to a storage tank and back; temperature differences cause the water to flow. This storage tank can be hooked up to a conventional water heater as a pre-heater or can be the main hot water tank. With only a main tank, you'll still need an electric element or gas burner to heat water on cloudy days. The typical cost for passive hot water systems runs in the $8,000 to $10,000 range, before figuring in tax credits and incentives that can lop off thousands of dollars from your final cost.

Active systems are more sophisticated. They use a pump to circulate the water from flat plate or evacuated-tube solar collectors to a heat exchanger or tank. An evacuated-tube system can heat up to 100 gallons per day, which makes it suitable to tie into a home's radiant heating system for even bigger savings. Depending on the home size, active solar systems that heat water and provide radiant heating will typically cost $18,000 to $25,000 installed. Again, your final cost depends on what tax credits and incentives are available in your area. Also, in most areas the payback—the final cost of the install minus credits, divided by the monthly energy savings—is currently running between five and twelve years.

To maintain a home's comfort level, the twin of capturing solar gain for heating in winter is cooling the home in summer. Energy efficient cooling, like heating, begins with good design. Shading eves, floor plans that allow cooling breezes to circulate, and the home's orientation, for example, help keep summer temperatures comfortable.

Of course, good design can only go so far, and most areas still need a mechanical cooling system that kicks in on the hottest days. One energy efficient system that combines both heating and cooling capabilities is a ground-source heat pump, sometimes called a geothermal system. This sys-

tem can be adapted to work with work with heat pumps, forced-air furnaces, hot-water systems, and radiant floor-heating systems.

Essentially, geothermal systems collect heat from water that circulates
through underground plastic pipe. Because temperatures several feet underground stay fairly constant (about 55 degrees) throughout the year, you can
cool in the summer and heat in the winter from this thermal reservoir. You
can even boost efficiency by installing pipes in water wells, ponds, swimming pools, vertical shafts, and extended runs in large yards.

Paired with a heat pump, a ground-source loop can cut energy costs to
about half, depending on location and climate. Costs typically run 50 to 80
percent higher than a standard heat pump or gas furnace with central air,
about $12,000 to $18,000 depending on house size and site. Tax credits
and/or incentives will reduce these costs significantly. Compared to standard gas or electric heating systems, payback would likely be twelve to
eighteen years. When you estimate payback using current energy prices,
twelve to eighteen years is probably too conservative, because if trends continue, energy costs are certain to continue rising.

Installing Green Insulation

How well you insulate your home is closely tied to the importance of the
efficiency of heating and cooling systems. Green insulation is a top design
priority, because heating and cooling account for over half of a home's
energy use.

 Here are some insulation information sites:

www.ornl.gov/sci/roofs+walls/insulation/ins_01.html

www.rvalue.net/

www.energystar.gov/index.cfm?c=home_sealing.hm_
improvement_ insulation_table

www.eere.energy.gov/consumer/your_home/insulation_airsealing/
index.cfm/mytopic=11370

www.ftc.gov/bcp/conline/pubs/alerts/rvaluealrt.shtm

A tight, well insulated building is critical to an energy efficient home.

And to make it easier, more green insulation products are appearing on the market that don't give off toxic gasses—mainly formaldehyde—though you have to hunt for them. For example, most new homes are sheathed with oriented-strand-board (OSB) panels that have a rigid insulation layer and foil barrier attached. It's an effective product, but unfortunately the adhesives used in making it may give off formaldehyde gas. Many other insulation products give off the same gas or cause environmental problems during manufacture, so do some homework and make sure the products you're considering are safe and made from renewable products, such as cellulose.

But there's more to your home's protective envelope than just insulation. Barriers that block air and water vapor from entering the home are equally important. The two need to work together as a system to keep out water vapor that can condense and cause rot and mold.

As with most products, there are trade-offs on which insulation is your best choice. Insulation typically comes in four types:

1. *Batts*: Although fiberglass—the yellow or pink rolls of fiberglass products you see at home centers—is the biggest seller in the batt market, recycled cotton, wood, and mineral wool are also available. Installing batts appears deceptively easy, but leaving gaps or careless cutting or fitting can allow cold air and/or vapor to infiltrate. If water vapor condenses on a barrier, that can cause rot or mold.

2. *Blown-in insulation*: Cellulose and fiberglass blown into roof and wall cavities do a good job of filling those tough-to-reach spots, which batt installers can miss. Blown-in insulation is also a low-density product with lots of air pockets, like a down-filled parka. Cellulose, which has an R-factor of 3.5 per inch, compared to 2.5 for fiberglass, absorbs and releases moisture, unlike fiberglass. Because cellulose is made from recycled paper, it's a good choice for green homebuilders.

3. *Sprayed in foam*: This insulation has two components, which are mixed at the nozzle as it's sprayed into place. The foam expands upon application and quickly cures into a solid, creating an efficient air and water vapor barrier that can have a high R factor. There are two types of foam, open and closed cell. Open-cell foam has an R-value of 3.6 per inch and uses water as a blowing agent. Closed-cell foam uses pentane (a hydrocarbon) as a blowing agent, but has an R-value of about 5 per inch. Foams are the most expensive home insulation products and can cost over $6.00 a square foot.

They are not a do-it-yourself application; trained installers and equipment are necessary for a quality job. And you'll need to do some homework before deciding on a product, because not all foams are environmentally friendly, either in installation or manufacture.

4. *Rigid board insulation*: This type of insulation is primarily used under concrete slabs and wall and roof sheathing. In residential construction, three kinds of rigid foam boards are commonly used: expanded polystyrene (EPS), extruded polystyrene (XPS), and polyisocyanurate (polyiso). EPS has the lower R-value, about 4 per inch, and costs about 40 cents a square foot for a 1-inch thick panel. Its primary use is to insulate concrete forms (ICFs) and structural insulated panels (SIPs) used in roof and foundation insulation. XPS has an R-value of about 5 per inch, which makes it a better insulator than EPS; it costs about 52 cents per square foot. It's used as sheathing in walls, roofs, and basement walls. Polyiso panels have the highest R-value of around 6. Cost is about 62 cents per square foot. These panels are usually manufactured with aluminum or fiberglass facing, and polyiso's main advantage over EPS and XPS is better heat resistance.

It's important to note that although these products are widely used and highly effective, they're made from hydrocarbons—the same material in Styrofoam coffee cups. You may want to discuss with your green architect or builder what alternative products they suggest for your area. Also, when you pair high efficiency insulation with advanced framing methods that use engineered wood products rather than standard lumber, you gain in two ways. First, you make more efficient use of forest products, and second, engineered wood is more efficient than standard lumber, so you can use less wood and more insulation, reducing energy loss.

The common measure of insulation effectiveness is the R-value; the higher the number, the better the thermal performance. For instance, in colder areas minimum attic insulation should be R-38, with R-19 for the walls. An inch of insulation, depending on the type, typically has an R-factor range between 2.3 and 7.

Some green insulation products you may want to seriously consider are:

- Cellulose made from shredded newsprint and cotton products that are energy efficient to produce.

- Polyurethane foam (SPF) that uses a water-based spray.

- BioBased Systems' soy insulation, made up of soybean oil-based polyurethane.

- Bonded-Logic's insulation made from denim that is treated with borate to give it fire-retardant and mold-resistant qualities.

- Many fiberglass insulation manufacturers are also incorporating recycled materials into their products. For example, CertainTeed and Owens Corning have products certified by the GreenGuard Environmental Institute (www.greenguard.org) for low emissions of formaldehyde and other pollutants.

VENTILATING YOUR NEW HOME

Prior to the 1960s, the dark ages of home building, high efficiency insulation, vapor barriers or house wraps, and low E windows didn't exist. Homes were not very tight, and air infiltrated under doors and through windows and dozens of cracks. You could cook with garlic and onions and the odors didn't stay around long enough to cause problems.

Once builders started to wrap homes in water- and air-tight materials, the rules changed. Homes no longer breathed, so ventilation systems were needed to introduce fresh air.

Causes of Poor Air Quality

Once you wrap a home in an air-tight insulated envelope, it's like living in a huge plastic bag. Although you won't die from lack of oxygen, the buildup of pollutants can affect your health. This results in the perception held by some home buyers that modern homes can make you sick. In fact, the Environmental Protection Agency lists poor indoor air quality among its top environmental threats.

The top indoor pollutants are:

- Smoke from tobacco, cooking, frying, and aerosols are common sources.

- VOCs (volatile organic compounds) are some of the most common chemicals contaminating indoor air. Examples include formaldehyde, synthetic carpet, and oil-based paint.

- Particles shed from pets, dust mites, mold, and other critters can cause allergic reactions and asthma.

Incorporating a Whole-House Ventilation System into Plans for Your Home

You certainly don't want to return to the days of leaky, drafty, cold houses. Luckily, there are several things you can do to ventilate a home to solve many potential health problems and get a supply of fresh air. One of the best solutions is a whole-house ventilation system.

Essentially this system is a central exhaust fan connected by ducts to vents in different parts of the home. The system also has two or more ingress vents to supply fresh air. Coupled with separate vents in bathrooms and the kitchen, the system can control moisture and indoor pollution.

If you live in a humid area, whole-house ventilation is critical to controlling mold and wood rot. A few extra hundred dollars spent making sure you have a good system is not an expense; it's an investment.

Since you're building a new home, you can incorporate a state-of-art whole-house ventilation system with the latest quiet fan technology into your design. These fans can run continuously, be hooked up to timers, or manually controlled. Advantages of these systems are:

- Every room in the house is vented, and air circulates to avoid concentrations of moist air that can cause mold growth.

- Indoor pollution that can cause respiratory problems and a sick house doesn't build up.

- Fresh air and exhaust vents can incorporate heat exchangers that prevent warm air from venting and cold air from cooling the house.

- When additional bathroom, laundry, and range vents are added, the house becomes healthy and more comfortable.

How you configure these whole-house systems and auxiliary vents depends on where you live, the size of the home, and the local climate.

In addition to venting, changes in your lifestyle can reduce pollutants. For example:

Research the products you use, such as carpets, paint, cleaning supplies, etc., and use only certified green products.

Don't burn candles, and use aerosols sparingly.

Cook only when a kitchen fan vented to the outside is running.

Run bathroom fans whenever you're showering to prevent excess humidity from building up.

Home Ventilation Standards

Because house venting is now such an important aspect of our health and happiness, the American Society of Heating, Refrigerating, and Air-Conditioning Engineers (www.ashrae.org) has come up with a recommended home ventilation standard, ASHRAE 62.2. Their recommendations include:

- Minimum whole house ventilation of 45 cubic feet per minute (cfm) for a two or three bedroom home up to 1,500 square feet; 60 cfm for homes up to 3,000 square feet; and 75 cfm for a larger four- or five-bedroom home up to 3,000 square feet.

- In addition to whole-house ventilation, a vented range hood in the kitchen with a minimum of 100 cfm, or a fan that can make five air changes per hour.

- Bathroom fans must be capable of at least 50 cfm, or there must be a continuously operating 20-cfm exhaust fan.

- The home must have pleated furnace filters (MERV 6 or better), or a more aggressive filtration system, if needed.

The bottom line to designing today's tight homes is to make sure you install an aggressive ventilation and filter system to keep indoor air pollution at a minimum.

DETERMINING WHETHER SOLAR OR WIND POWER ARE FOR YOU

At some point after you've worked through the insulation, heating, and cooling, and ventilation phases of designing your dream home, your thoughts may turn to more exciting aspects of a green home. And if you're like most homeowners, adding the ability to generate your own power is an enticing idea. You can become energy independent. No more power company with its black-outs, brown-outs, and increasing rates. But, as with any other technology, there are trade-offs as well as pros and cons.

For most homeowners, generating their own power doesn't mean cutting ties to their local power company—not when the utility offers *net metering*. You'll hear this term a lot when wind or solar power is discussed. It means that any excess power generated by your system is purchased by the power company. In other words, when your system is generating excess power, your meter runs backwards. Cool!

Net metering, along with tax rebates and state, local, and utility incentives, can make generating your own power economically feasible. However, incentives differ widely depending on what area of the country you live in. So, the first step in your feasibility study is find out what resources are available to you in your area. Some sources to check out are:

- Look for federal, state, and local tax rebates. It's likely you'll end up with three levels of rebates that can make solar or wind power even more enticing. Two helpful Web sites are: www.findsolar.com/index.php?page=taxcredit and www.dsireusa.org for a database of state-by-state incentives. Don't overlook your city government for incentives and credits, either.

- Local suppliers of solar power equipment usually stay current on incentives in their service area because they use the info in their sales pitches.

- Contact your local power company for their policy on net metering.

- Make sure your solar or wind installation won't violate zoning or neighborhood covenants.

Like any other major project, get at least three bids on a complete solar system, installed and producing power. Compare bids and go with the one you feel will give you the best product for the money.

Generating Solar Power

Typically, to generate solar power, you should plan on 1 kilowatt (1,000 watts) per 1,000 square feet of house area. However, grid efficiency depends on location. A solar system in Maine will differ from one in New Mexico.

Along with solar panels, you'll need an inverter to convert the direct current (DC) produced by the solar panels to the alternating current (AC) power used by your home's electrical system and the utility company.

Two other terms you'll encounter in solar power circles are *grid-tied* and *off the grid*. Grid-tied means you are connected to your local power company and can draw power or sell power back to them when you have excess (net metering).

Off the grid refers to systems that are not hooked up to the local power company. When days are bright and sunny, generated power is stored in deep-cycle batteries. At night and on cloudy days, the home's electrical system draws power from the batteries. A three-kilowatt system could require as many as sixteen batteries. If you live in an area with lots of cloudy days, you may also need a backup generator.

Depending on where you live, a solar system will cost anywhere from $20,000 to $35,000 installed and producing power. Rebates and incentives could reduce this to by 40 to 50 percent.

When you divide the monthly power savings into the total cost of the system, you'll typically reach a breakeven point in twelve to eighteen years. However, this time frame doesn't take into account any ongoing incentives, property value increases, and utility rate increases.

Generating Wind Power

Trade a wind turbine generator for solar panels and you may be able to generate enough power to run your home and possibly even net-metering. Wind-powered generators, like solar panels, generate DC electricity that converts to AC with an inverter.

If your system is on-grid, you can sell excess power to the local utility; off the grid, you'll need batteries to store power when it's not so windy.

The ideal location for a wind turbine is twenty feet above any surrounding object within a 250-foot radius. This generally means your property should be at least half an acre or larger to effectively site the turbine. For many homeowners this can represent a problem that solar panels don't have.

Cost wise, wind power is roughly competitive to solar, depending on location and, of course, how heavy the winds blow at your building site.

Here are some wind power Web sites:

www.awea.org/faq/smsyslst.html

www.poweredgenerators.com/wind-power-generators.html

www.eere.energy.gov/windandhydro/wind_how.html

USING SUSTAINABLE PRODUCTS AND CUTTING COSTS

Many homeowners find that after they've gotten the mechanics—power, insulation, windows, and other heavy duty items—past the design stage, finding and shopping for sustainable products such as paint, counter-tops, appliances, floor coverings, and so on becomes the fun part of their project.

This is where can let your creativity roam free. Homeowners have used bamboo, recycled glass, concrete, non-endangered wood species, and dozens of other products in new and exciting ways that save forests and petroleum resources.

Doing the Up-Front Work

If you're like most green homeowners, the reason you want to build your own home is to save energy and do your part in saving the environment. To achieve those worthy goals you need to do some up-front work. This may include:

- Researching the products you plan to use to make sure they are truly sustainable and don't add to the problem in the way they're manufactured, transported, or used.

- Making sure at the end of a product's life span it doesn't end up as toxic landfill and can be recycled or safely reused.

- Focusing on finding local products whenever possible. Trucking green materials long distances can negate the reason we're using them in the first place.

- Using recyclable materials whenever possible. Wood from old buildings can often be used for floors, cabinets, furniture—wherever your imagination takes you. Glass can be recycled into tiles, counter tops, and other products that enterprising recyclers devise.

- Choosing the most energy efficient appliances and fixtures possible. They may cost a little more up-front, but that cost is usually more than recouped over the appliance's lifespan.

- Checking out salvage yards, pre-demo sales for building materials and fixtures, second-hand stores, classified ads, and Web sites.

Handling the Trade-Offs

Handling the trade-offs is one of the biggest challenges in building a green home. For many new homeowners, it comes down to budget versus green products. You can't always go with the greenest product you would like. Few homeowners can sit down with a builder or architect, plan their dream home, and move in three to six months later.

For most homeowners who have a passion to create a green home, it becomes a journey, a work in progress that may span years. But as one homebuilding couple said of their green home, "It took us nine years to complete our dream home the way we wanted it, but it was worth it; we had so much fun along the way."

So, how do you decide on trade-offs? Some suggestions are:

• Create a budget for the different components of your project. You'll likely need to involve your architect and/or builder up-front so you know how to allocate the costs realistically.

• Start with the total project amount minus 15 percent set aside for unforeseen costs (yes, you'll always have unforeseen costs; yes, you'll always use the reserve).

• Fund the important big ticket items first, such as foundation, framing, sheathing, insulation, windows, roof, and so on.

• If you need to cut costs, defer some projects until later. For example, add power- or hot water-generating solar panels later on, or go with a heating system that can be upgraded to a geothermal system.

• Go with used appliances that you can replace later.

• Find used lighting and bathroom fixtures that you can replace with green ones as soon as funds permit.

• Seek out and talk to other green homeowners for tips and ideas on how they solved problems building their homes. The creativity of people working around challenges they encounter is amazing.

AVOIDING THE SEVEN BIGGEST MISTAKES THAT MANY NEW GREEN HOMEOWNERS MAKE

To help you navigate the process of building your green home, here are the seven biggest mistakes that new homeowners make that frequently cost them time, money, and frustration. Avoid them!

1.   Not taking the time to research your building lot before committing. Do some homework before you get serious about a building site. Some suggestions are:

- Look at the local schools (good schools add to value).

- Make sure you know how the home will sit on the lot in relation to other homes, especially those that have not yet started construction. Verify that you have the southern exposure you need for solar gain.

- Look for geological and environmental hazards, such as building on an earthquake fault or in a canyon full of trees or undergrowth that can become a fire hazard.

- Check out the zoning and look for any planned changes that will impact your site.

2.   Shop for location and community first. You don't want to move into your new home and find out you don't like the neighbors or they don't share your values. Make sure you don't end up with a killer commute or that the distance to the kid's soccer lessons, school location, and your work will create a scheduling nightmare.

- Check out the demographics of the neighborhood before you commit. If you're the only one serious about a green home, you may be happier finding neighbors who share your environmental views.

- Walk around and talk to several homeowners in the area you're considering before you write a deposit check on a lot. If there are problems with the developer or builder, you want to know about them up-front.

3. If you're building in a new green community, read the builder's contract carefully, or have an attorney look at it before you sign. Look for clauses that don't allow you to hire a third-party home inspector before closing. And no, a walk-through with the builder before closing doesn't cut it. If you knew what to look for, you would be building the home.

Some other paperwork must-dos are:

- Everything needs to be in writing; no exceptions.

- In the final walk-through, get a written punch list (a list of problems the builder needs to correct) and make sure they're completed before closing.

- If possible, talk to some new homeowners on the street and ask how the contractor handled their punch lists and what callbacks they had before you sign a contract.

- Get copies of all warranties from the builder, especially on solar power and hot water systems, windows, roofs, and other hi-tech systems. You should end up with a stack of them. It's important to organize them in a file along with dated purchase receipts in case you need warranty work on a collector, pump, or other item.

4. It's important to find a buyers' agent who specializes in new green homes. An experienced and knowledgeable agent is a valuable resource for guiding you through the maze of finding a lot and building a new home. The builder usually pays the agent's fee, so it's free to you. In finding a buyer's agent:

- Get recommendations from other new green homebuyers in the area.

- Interview at least three before making a choice.

- Look at the agent's new home sales track record and experience working with green home buyers.

- Don't choose an agent because he or she is a relative, friend of a friend, etc. Choose one like you would a brain surgeon.

5. Not having your financing pre-approved before going shopping is a common mistake many buyers make. Sometimes builders have an in-

house lender who offers incentives if you go with them. Don't assume this is the best deal. Get a good faith estimate (GFE) and compare it with the one from your lender. Sometimes it's a better deal, sometimes it isn't. Be sure to:

- Look at the closing costs each lender charges.

- Compare the Annual Percentage Rates (APR) on the GFEs. The lowest is usually the best deal.

- Make sure all the inspection fees are covered and energy credits are given if you're getting a green mortgage.

6.   Crystallize your plans and options up-front; get it all in writing and stay with it. Changing your mind after the home is underway and adding change orders is the single biggest budget buster (and builder's profit center) for most new homeowners. This is especially true when owners want to add high tech energy-saving systems after construction has started.

7.   Items that many new homeowners forget to get in writing are:

- Detailed sweat equity agreements. These agreements are important. Make sure what, when, and how much money is credited each time you work on the job. You may want to use a detailed worksheet that both you and the builder initial whenever you've completed any work.

- All builder's claims and promises, which should detail (in writing) what is included and not included and be verified.

- The make and model of the appliances the builder is installing, which should be in writing. If substitutions are made, you want to be in on it.

For most new green homeowners, the next challenge after moving in is landscaping their home site so that it's environmentally friendly and saves resources. Chapter 6 gives you tips on how to do that and save a few bucks, too.

CHAPTER 6

GREEN LANDSCAPING

Whether you're putting in landscaping for a new home or redoing your existing yard to be more environmentally sustainable and water efficient, this chapter shows you how. With recent unpredictable climate changes, areas that haven't before experienced water shortages are now enduring drought conditions—just ask the folks in Atlanta. Suddenly, water conservation strategies, efficient methods of collecting and storing rain or snowmelt, choosing drought-resistant plants, and using fewer toxic chemicals have become important aspects of mainstream landscaping.

Some of the "new" ideas, such as water recycling and collecting it in barrels and cisterns, are not strangers to the arid West and Southwest; the early settlers developed them out of necessity. We're dusting off many old conservation practices, such as planting trees to shade the house in summer and to serve as winter windbreaks, to cut down on energy use.

There's an upside to green landscaping—getting homeowners more involved with their yard and landscaping. Fewer new homeowners are now opting for contractor landscaping, where they typically plant a few trees, roll out a couple of thousand square feet of grass sod, add a few hundred feet of curbing with bark filling, and call it done.

Instead, owners are searching for water-efficient landscaping plants and learning how to landscape without thirsty Kentucky Blue (or similar grass type) lawns. Depending on the area, this can mean forgoing expanses of lawn and thirsty exotic plants in favor of landscaping with rocks, sand, and more drought-tolerant plants.

When establishing a new yard, you have the advantage of planning holistically from the beginning. You can design your yard and house to work harmoniously with your local environment.

However, if you're converting an existing yard to a greener one, you will find that it not only takes planning, but often requires replacing the present landscaping. A sustained effort over several years may be necessary to achieve the results you want, but it's worth it, for both you and the environment.

Successfully creating and living with green landscaping entails becoming involved and knowledgeable in several areas. Accordingly, in this chapter you'll learn how to create a green yard, either from scratch or by redoing an existing one, by:

1. Creating an action plan for an attractive landscape

2. Working with the characteristics of your soil

3. Determining where and what plants to use

4. Planning a sustainable landscape

5. Applying and conserving water

CREATING A LANDSCAPE ACTION PLAN

A big part of a home's value and curb appeal comes from attractive and well-maintained landscaping. Trees and shrubs provide privacy, summer shade, and shields against wind and snow, in addition to screening out unwanted views or providing a frame for desirable vistas. Landscaping boils down to using plants and structures to accentuate the positive aspects of your yard and downplay the problem areas.

However, many homeowners landscape their yard with large expanses of lawn and plants not suited to the local climate. This practice consumes increasingly scarce water resources. When coupled with overuse of herbicides, pesticides, fertilizers, and other toxic chemicals, unintended consequences result.

Using Xeriscaping Principles

To combat these problems, *xeriscaping practices* have received a lot of publicity in the past few years. Many people still believe xeriscaping means converting one's yard into sand, rocks, and scraggly bushes. Fortunately, this is more misunderstanding than reality.

To put us all on the same page, xeriscaping principles are based on:

- Creating a landscape design that integrates water conservation into the overall plan

- Reducing water-intensive turf and plants

- Using an environmentally sensible approach to soil improvement

- Selecting plants more suited to the local climate

- Utilizing mulch effectively to reduce water loss and soil erosion

- Using environmentally friendly fertilizers and pest control

As you can see, xeriscaping is more than sand and rocks, it brings conservation and environmental responsibility to landscaping and yard maintenance.

Planning a Landscape

If you don't have the time or inclination to become a green thumb (and many people don't), it would be a good investment to seek out and hire a landscape architect who shares your vision of an environmentally friendly yard. You can arrange for a complete project, ready for your lawn chairs, or contract for only those areas you don't want to handle on your own. But first, you need a plan.

Drawing a scale map of your lot on a large sheet of graph paper (one square equals one foot, for instance) or using a landscaping software program is the best way to start. If you would rather work from a computer screen, www.landscaping-software-review.toptenreviews.com is a Web site that compares several landscaping programs. Some of these programs allow you to rotate the lot plan, project it in 3-D, move items around, add different kinds of plants, and do all sorts of interesting things.

A detailed plan on paper or onscreen makes it easier to coordinate what plants you want and where to put them, as well as estimate the quantity and cost of materials needed.

Here are some suggestions for creating a detailed plan:

1.   Start by drawing a base plan of the property. It should include property lines, the house's footprint, driveways, walks, ponds, trees, and other existing features. You may have a deed map or plat that came with your title paperwork when you bought the property that provides the lot dimensions.

2.   Orient the plan so true north is at the top of the paper (see chapter 5 for how to find true north). Deed maps and plats are usually oriented with true north at the top of the page.

3.   Show the directions of prevailing winds and sun/shade patterns from trees or buildings.

4.   Note drainage patterns on your plan. To get accurate info on drainage, walk around your yard with an umbrella during a heavy rainstorm and note where the water is going.

5.   Determine which views you need to block, as well which views you want to preserve or accent.

6.   Pencil your various landscaping ideas on tracing paper overlays until you find what you like. It may take several attempts before you get close to what you want. Take the best ideas and then draw a final plan to use when you start moving dirt or to help communicate your vision for your green yard to a landscaping architect.

After you have a working landscape plan on either paper or your hard drive, the next step is to consider where to place the different elements (plants, trees, paths, lawn, and so on) of your landscaping.

Utilizing Seven Design Elements of Eco-Friendly Landscaping

How many times have you stopped in front of a yard to admire the landscaping? Everything fits—the colors coordinate, scale and proportions are just right, and it appears to blend into the natural surroundings. So why do some yards beckon you to stay awhile, relax, and enjoy while others don't?

Landscaping that attracts typically utilizes seven design elements:

1.   The first element is composition. As in award-winning paintings or photos, all the components appear to fit together in harmony. Likewise, in landscaping, trees, shrubs, lawn, and flowerbeds should fit together naturally. Composition, then, is how the landscaper frames the different components and groups into an overall landscaping plan.

2.   Balance is the next element of landscaping design. When you're looking at a yard that is out of balance, it feels as though something is missing or out of place. It could be that a tree grouping is in the wrong place, or flowerbeds are too small or too large for their location. Structures, fences, driveways, and the way the home sits on the lot can also appear unbalanced.

3.   Closely related to balance is scale, the third design element. Every feature in a landscape plan must be in proper scale in relation to the other features. For example, a small house dwarfed by large trees would be out of scale, as would a flowerbed too large or too small for the yard size. Homeowners often create scale problems in their yard when they don't anticipate the mature height of trees and shrubs or plant them too close to the house.

4.   Proportion is the fourth design element. The Greeks and Romans were masters of proportion; their buildings and landscaping used a 3/5 ratio (1.618) that is psychologically pleasing to most people. This ratio, often called the *golden mean*, also often occurs in the natural world (see http://goldennumber.net). When we use this ratio in landscaping by grouping plants, trees, and flowerbeds in threes or fives, we create a pleasing proportion. For example, if you have a 1,000-square-foot front yard that is now lawn and want to reduce water consumption by putting in a native flowerbed, what size should it be? Assuming you wanted to convert about a third, or, say, 375 square feet, the dimensions would be 15 feet by 25 feet, using the 3/5 rule.

5.   Color is also an important aspect of landscaping. An all-green or brown yard would be boring to look at and might create a marketing problem. A good starting place for bringing color to landscaping is planting colorful foundation, border, and groundcover plants. Even xeriscaping requires color and variety to create interest. Window boxes, flowering container

plants, interesting landscaping structures, among other things can liven up low-water yards.

6. A vital design element, often overlooked, is texture. You want to group similarly textured plants together. For example, normally you wouldn't plant a fine-textured plant like a red leaf maple next to a sharp-needled scrub pine. Texture is also an important consideration when you combine plants in containers or enclosures or next to fences or structures.

7. When you incorporate the previous design elements, the result is harmony, the seventh element. If you walk through a garden or yard and want to linger and enjoy it, you are experiencing harmony. It's one of those you-know-it-when-you-see-it feelings, and you don't get that feeling if all the design elements are not in harmony.

There is probably no such thing as the perfect yard. Distracting views, utility boxes, nearby buildings, and other problems can pose landscaping challenges. To solve these problems, include such elements on your base site plan, along with notes on how they affect the current landscape.

Next, brainstorm various solutions on overlays or a computer screen until you find an idea that can work. It's easier to work it out on paper than changing landscaping. See the sidebar for Web sites with helpful design tips.

 Interesting Landscaping Web Sites

www.the-landscape-design-site.com/

www.landscaping.about.com/cs/designexamples1/a/landscapeDesign.htm

www.edis.ifas.ufl.edu/MG086

www.mylandscapingexpert.com/

www.landscapingideasonline.com/

Considering Whether to Hire a Professional Designer or Landscaper

If designing and putting in landscaping is competing with fishing, golfing, or anything else you would rather do, then hiring a landscaping designer may be the best way to go. This is an especially good investment if you have a challenging lot. Professionals spend every day solving landscaping problems the rest of us may see only once or twice a lifetime.

Probably the biggest reason to invest in professional landscaping services is that how your yard looks has a big impact on your home's value. If you don't have a green thumb, investing in a professional design can yield a return many times the cost.

Here's an example of how landscaping adds to home value. When Wes and Carol decided to retire and move to a warmer Arizona climate, they put their home of twelve years on the market. They both loved to work in the yard, which was the envy of the neighborhood. Wide flowerbeds with drip irrigation lines bordered the yard, and trees framed the home. The owners had installed four fifty-gallon white oak barrels at each corner of the house to capture rain for watering their well-tended garden. Of course, the lawn was lush and green even during the hot summer months because the owners knew how and when to water and mow, and they used organic fertilizers.

Although it was a slow market, with many similarly priced homes for sale, the first couple who looked at the home made a full price offer. That the home was in great condition and decorated nicely was important, but the yard closed the deal, according to the buyers at closing. They didn't want to risk losing it by making a low offer.

Because attractive landscaping is so important to a home's value and curb appeal, it's wise to budget for landscaping in your initial estimates. If funds are short and/or you don't have a green thumb, some options are:

- Hire a landscape designer to do the plans. Do the work yourself, or hire out the work that you can't or don't want to handle.

- Hire out the grunt work—moving dirt and installing curbing and lawn— if you have design skills and can create the plans.

- Hire a landscaping firm that can both design and install.

- Take landscaping classes at local colleges or universities, and put in the yard yourself.

However, if you can fit it into your budget, hiring a professional landscape designer to work with you on your plans is recommended.

Using a professional is especially recommended if you plan to xeriscape your yard. Many homeowners who choose to go this route feel it's an easier and cheaper way to landscape their yard. Actually, the opposite is true. To create an attractive xeriscaped yard takes a lot of experience and creativity because the expanses of water-hungry lawn and colorful plants many of us are used to working with are absent. That can be a challenge if you don't want your yard to look like a place where antelope roam.

Landscape design fees vary considerably. Typically, a full landscape design can cost a couple of hundred to a thousand dollars, depending on the complexity and the area you live in. Naturally, you'll want to shop around and get several bids; compare before you commit.

Hiring a professional landscape designer is similar to hiring an architect or builder. Build a list and interview the best three, and hopefully you'll find the one you want to hire.

Some suggestions for finding and hiring a designer and/or landscaping contractor include:

1. Ask homeowners whose yards you admire who did their yard design.

2. Check out local garden and landscaping clubs for referrals.

3. Choose a landscape architect who has a degree and belongs to a licensed professional association. It may cost slightly more, but you'll recoup the investment many times over.

4. Check out the designers' and contractors' credentials and references. Ask to see portfolios of previous jobs or for references you can contact.

5. Verify licenses and insurance coverage (workers' comp and liability) if you're hiring a landscaping contractor and get everything in writing.

6. Try to hire a designer or contractor in the less-busy off-season (fall or winter).

If you can't afford to do everything at once, begin with an overall plan and then install various components over time. Break the job down into manageable steps and do them as time and money allow. For example, you could install the fence and drip irrigation system this year, a water retention system next year, and a pond the third year.

Once you have identified the basics of what you want your yard to look like and have the design on paper or computer screen, the next step is to determine what type of soil you have to work with.

WORKING WITH YOUR SOIL'S CHARACTERISTICS

Your yard's soil quality compares to your home's foundation. If there are problems with the foundation, everything above it will also have problems. Likewise, identifying your soil's characteristics and what improvements it needs to support your landscaping plan is critical.

No two soils are alike; in fact, they can differ considerably within the same lot. You've likely seen green lawns with brown or dead patches, even though these areas are getting enough water. Possibly, the soil is compacted or has too much clay, so water can't penetrate to the root zone. If the soil is sandy, water passes through the root zone; nothing holds it long enough for the roots to absorb it.

Soils are broadly classified as mineral or organic. Mineral soils are usually young soils—decomposing rock that has not had a chance to mix with sand and organic matter. Organic soils are older soils that have had plants and organisms growing in them for some time and have collected a lot of organic matter. This mix of mineral and organic material is what makes up the soil's texture. For optimum growing, soils should contain both mineral and organic materials.

Organic material, or decaying plant and animal matter in the soil, is what gives it the ability to retain and make water available to root systems. How much organic matter is in the soil matrix is a critical measure of how well your plants will grow.

There are two ways to add minerals to the soil. The recommended method is with organic products, such as chicken or cow manure. Another, unfortunately popular, method is to spread chemicals in granular or liquid form, which can prove toxic to microorganisms, beneficial insects, and earthworms. We hope you'll lean toward the organic solution.

Getting to Know Your Soil

How available nutrients are to a plant depends on how acid or alkaline the soil is. The measuring stick for this is the pH scale, from 0 to 14. Less than seven is on the acid side and above seven is alkaline. Soils with a high amount of organic material tend to be acidic, or lower than seven.

Some plants prefer acid soils, while others grow better in slightly alkaline soil.

You can change the pH of your soil with additives, but that requires additional maintenance and resources. It's usually better to go with plants that do well in your native soil. For example, if you wanted to grow rhododendrons that thrive in rainy Washington State in your garden in the Nevada desert, you'd need to make some big changes. The soil would need conditioning and additives to make it acidic, and the plants would likely need frequent watering as well as having a mister going most of the time to counter the desert's 4 to 10 percent summer humidity.

Many owners try to force their landscaping into something their local climate and soil won't support, resulting in a waste of resources. Xeriscaping is all about going native to conserve water and resources.

Determining Your Soil's pH

To determine the pH level in your soil, you can:

- Take soil samples to a private testing laboratory in your area. Check your local phone book under Soil Testing.

- Check with larger nurseries, they may do soil testing or can refer you to a lab that does.

- The U.S. Department of Agriculture (USDA) has county extension offices that can direct you. For the office nearest you, go to www.usda.gov/extension.

 Additional soil testing info Web sites are:

http://hgic.clemson.edu/factsheets/hgic1652.htm

ohioline.osu.edu/hyg-fact/1000/1132.html

www.soilperfect.com/

www.timberleafsoiltesting.com/

www.heirloomseeds.com/soil.htm

Once you've identified your soil's texture and pH, you can take the steps needed to optimize its plant growing potential. In most cases, this will mean aerating or breaking up the soil and mixing in organic material to enhance its nutrient value and help it retain water.

For example, if the soil is too acid, you can add powered limestone, available from most garden nurseries. However, if it's alkaline—sometimes caused by poor drainage—you'll need to mix in lots of organic material and create good drainage to leach out any salts.

Local nurseries and your county USDA extension office are excellent resources on soils in your area. If you're working with a landscape designer, she will know what soil and plant options are best for your area and climate. Other sources you may check out are local garden clubs, USDA publications, and suggestions from others who have attractive xeriscaped yards.

DETERMINING WHERE AND WHAT TO PLANT, AND LANDSCAPING MISTAKES TO AVOID

Unless you hire a local professional landscaper to help pick out plants for your yard, you'll need to do some homework. A successful landscape depends on plants that are right for your climate and soil type. Oddly enough, microclimates and different soil types that affect which plants will grow can change dramatically within a small area. That makes it important to look for these anomalies and note them on your plot plan.

Common microclimates that can affect your plant choices are:

- Soils and airflow on top of hills, which often differ from valley sites, affect which plants will thrive.

- Building sites midway down slopes commonly have different soils and less exposure. You can sometimes grow plants on a hillside that you can't in the valley below.

- Building sites in valley bottoms or at the mouth of canyons may have cold air patterns that limit what you can grow.

- Nearby lakes, ponds, and rivers can influence what plants grow best on your site.

- Proximity to hills, mountains, buildings, trees, and so on can limit sunlight and the growing capacities of your building site.

If you have green-thumb neighbors, check with them about what plants do well and which ones don't. The more data you can collect on which local plants succeed, the easier it'll be for you to create a successful yard.

Note all this information on your plot plan so you can start planning for the types of trees and other plants that have proven successful in your area. Next, determine where to locate trees, flowerbeds, edging, and lawns. You may go through a few overlays if you're using graph paper, but that's better than planting a tree in the wrong place. At this point, it may be helpful to review the seven design principles covered earlier in Utilizing Seven Design Elements of Eco-Friendly Landscaping.

Also, beware of these five mistakes do-it-yourselfers often make while landscaping their yards:

1. When planting trees and large shrubs, many homeowners don't factor in the mature size on their plan. The result is trees or bushes planted too close to the house or too close together. After a few years, the growing trees compromise the yard's scale and balance.

2. Not taking the time to grade the lot so rain and melt water flows away from the home's foundation is an expensive mistake. To make sure you avoid this problem, walk around the yard during a heavy rain storm and observe where the water flows.

3. Don't neglect the important step of grading the lawn bed for consistent soil quality and to avoid low or high spots. Low spots puddle and kill the lawn; high spots don't retain water or fertilizer and end up with dead grass.

4. Planting trees in front of the house rather than to frame it is a common error. Landscaping should accent and show off the house, not hide it. If you stand in front of a home, the landscaping should draw your eye to an attractive entryway.

5. Planting trees, shrubs, and other plants before homeowners research them to make sure they are compatible with the local climate (microclimate) and are water efficient is yet another common mistake that can be avoided.

Many nurseries offer knowledgeable design and plant people who will work with you on your landscaping plan free when you buy their stock. This can be especially helpful if the nursery specializes in xeriscaping or indigenous plants.

PLANNING A SUSTAINABLE LANDSCAPE

The key to sustainable landscaping is recycling organic matter through a three-step system that replenishes plant nutrients, conserves water, and improves soil texture. The components of this system are compost, mulch, and green fertilizer.

Essentially, your goal is to create a bio-world where worms, insects, and microorganisms break down (compost) leaves, lawn clippings, manure, and other biodegradable products into mulch and fertilizer that plants can use. Composting is a marvel of conservation and sustainability.

The Art of Composting

Compost is an important part of landscaping. When mixed with soil, the organic material from the compost pile not only improves it, but also increases its ability to retain water for plant use. When used as mulch or an organic top layer, it insulates soil from summer heat and reduces water loss through evaporation.

Composting is simple. All you need is some space to create a freestanding pile of organic materials, such as grass clippings, leaves, sawdust, or other biodegradable residue. The three important factors that allow the system to work at optimum levels are temperature, moisture, and air circulation.

Composing containers vary from four wood posts with wire mesh sides to fifty-gallon plastic drums mounted on frames so they can rotate. Check out the following Web site for ideas:

www.peoplepoweredmachines.com

www.composters.com

www.thegardenhelper.com/compost.html

www.clemson.edu/sandhill/page.htm?pageId=3097

www.maskedflowerimages.com/composting.html

Organic material in a pile or container will generate heat (120 to 130 degrees) as microorganisms break down the plant cellulose. If the center of your compost pile is generating heat, you know it's working.

Moisture is essential to the composting process because all those hard-at-work microorganisms require it for digestion. Ideally, the compost pile should be moist but not soaking wet. Air has to circulate throughout the pile.

Yes, all those little bugs chowing compost need to breathe too, at least the good ones we want to remain. Another type from the dark side, called anaerobic microorganisms, can live without oxygen. They can also break down compost but create offensive odors in the process that your neighbors won't appreciate.

To keep the anaerobic critters out of the compost pile, you need to turn it every day or two with a pitchfork so it will stay loose and aerated.

What to Feed Your Compost Pile

You want to keep all those microorganisms happy so they reduce your compost pile as quickly as possible to a state plants can use. The ideal compost mix for microorganisms is about thirty parts carbon material to one part nitrogen. Carbon is essential for energy and nitrogen for conversion into protein.

Compost-friendly materials high in carbon are:

- Shredded woody and dried plant material
- Leaves and twigs
- Shredded newspaper (use sparingly)
- Sawdust

Materials that add nitrogen to the compost mix are:

- Chicken, turkey, or cow manure
- Fresh grass clippings
- Non-meat kitchen wastes, such as vegetable peelings, coffee grounds, eggshells, and so on.

Depending on the material, climate, and temperature, compost can take between about a month and a year to break down to a usable form. If you use a tumbler-type composter, you can often reduce the time considerably.

The two keys to successful composting are to keep it moist and turn or mix it every few days.

As a green homeowner, one of first things you want to do after buying a building lot is set up a compost area away from construction traffic. Add leaves, lawn clippings, and other organic products, and keep it moist and aerated, so that in a few months when you're ready to put in landscaping you'll have a good supply of mulch on hand for soil prep and planting.

The Value of Mulch

Green landscapers and gardeners would have a hard time without mulch. It protects soil and plants from drying out and adds nutrients. The best mulch comes from your compost; spread it several inches thick around plants and use as a cover for soil you want to protect and improve.

Beware of using wood chips or other organic material that has not broken down in your compost pile for mulch. Fresh uncomposted material robs soil (and your plants) of nitrogen as it breaks down, or composts, in your flowerbed. If you choose to use bark as a decorative layer, add a layer of compost or fertilizer next to the soil, then add the bark. However, for plants that require little water, you may want to use little or no mulch to prevent root rot from trapped moisture.

Another great way to mulch is use a lawnmower with a mulching blade that cuts grass clippings finer than a regular blade. These clippings are not bagged but left in the grass to compost in place. Some gardeners claim that if you mow the lawn when it's about one and a half inches tall and leave the clippings, you don't have to add commercial fertilizers.

You can also buy decorative commercial mulches from chipped wood that do a good job of protecting plants and soil. However, they can take a long time to break down, which may or may not be a problem for your garden décor.

Fertilizers and How to Reduce the Need for Them

Fertilizers have taken a bad rap over the past few years. Careless over-application by homeowners and agriculture have contaminated our water resources and caused many environmental problems. As a result, it's important to mainly use organic fertilizers, which are more likely to remain in the soil and break down, rather than leach into the environment.

Depending on their source, fertilizers can be natural, synthetic, organic, or inorganic. Natural organic fertilizers come from animal or plant products, such a manure and compost. Synthetic organic products are processed natural products that may contain additives.

Inorganic fertilizers are mineral based, easily dissolve in water, and fast-acting. These are great if you need to green up a lawn quickly. However, there's an environmental price when they leach into lakes, rivers, and throughout the eco-system.

Typically, homeowners buy a couple of bags of inorganic fertilizer in the early spring and spread it on their lawn to get it to green up quickly. No one wants to be last on his block to have a green lawn.

But as a green homeowner, you take a different route. Natural fertilization is something you do all year long with organic products, not the three or four recommended applications printed on the back of a commercial fertilizer bag. True, the natural products are slow-acting and require a more hands-on approach and careful planning, but they're more environmentally friendly.

 Fertilizer Info Web sites:

www.howstuffworks.com/question181.htm

http://edis.ifas.ufl.edu/MG090

www.the-organic-gardener.com/organic-fertilizer.html

www.extremelygreen.com/fertilizerguide.cfm

Mycorrhizae is a fungus that lives on plant roots. Along with other microorganisms, it helps plants extract nutrients from the soil. Poor soil management, harmful chemicals, over-watering, and over-fertilizing harm these fungi and other organisms, so that plants don't grow as well.

On the other hand, green management practices encourage the growth of these little critters, along with earthworms and beneficial insects. Essentially, we're encouraging an interdependent mini bio-world that results in a two-way exchange. We manage it intelligently and it rewards us with abundance without the use of environmentally harmful chemicals.

Here are some of the things we can do to encourage the health of this bio-world:

- Check the soil's pH level at least once a year. If the soil is too alkaline (pH greater than 7), iron becomes chemically unavailable to many plant roots; your garden will do better if you select plants that can thrive in that type of soil. Conversely, if the soil is acidic, you'll want to select plants that thrive in that type of soil.

- Allow as much plant residue as practicable to stay on and in the soil and compost in place.

- Use a mulch blade on your mower and don't bag the clippings.

- Water carefully and only until moisture reaches the root zone. Overwatering leaches out important soil nutrients and wastes water.

- Sweep up grass clippings from sidewalks and driveways and add to the compost pile.

- Avoid the use of herbicide and fertilizer combinations.

- Don't use complete fertilizers. If you have a soil problem, have it tested and add only the deficient nutrient. Also, seek advice from a nursery or your county USDA agent.

- Encourage earthworms to take up residence in your soil. Few things help aerate and improve soil texture more than earthworms. Their droppings, called *castings* when deposited atop the ground, are rich in nitrogen, calcium, magnesium, and phosphorus. These are important nutrients for healthy ecosystems. For more info on earthworms, check out www. microsoil.com/earthworm.htm.

APPLYING AND CONSERVING WATER

As most of us have experienced, precipitation patterns around the country are erratic, and areas with typically high rainfall are experiencing drought conditions. Water restrictions have become mandatory for homeowners that have never experienced them before. As a result, we need to learn new skills to use the water we have more efficiently and to landscape with conservation in mind.

One of the best ways to conserve water is not to use the automatic timers on sprinkler system. Set the system to manual and then turn on only those areas that need water. True, it's convenient to set the timer for 4 a.m. every day or every other day and let the watering stations cycle through until sunup. But automatic watering is highly wasteful.

For example, a homeowner dug a hole for a four-inch by four-inch fence post in the lawn and noticed the soil was saturated down about two feet. He had set the timer on the sprinkler system to activate for one-half hour every morning at 5 a.m. Not only did the lawn turn into a sponge, but fertilizer and nutrients leached down beyond the root zone. The homeowner kept applying more and more fertilizer to keep the lawn green. Unfortunately, every summer across the country this scenario plays out in countless yards, wasting water and resources.

Lawn and garden watering info Web sites:

www.gardening.wsu.edu/library/lanb002/lanb002.htm

www.lewisgardens.com/watering.htm

www.cals.arizona.edu/pubs/garden/mg/arboriculture/watering.html

www.american-lawns.com/lawns/watering.html

www.ehow.com/how_812_water-lawn.html

Determining When to Water

Learning how plants react when they are over or under watered takes some effort. It's not astrophysics but a matter of observation and learning what to look for. It's interesting that homeowners kill more plants by overwatering than underwatering.

The following tips can help fine-tune water use.

• Wilt on broadleaf plants is an obvious indicator of water stress. But you should also look for dropping leaves and color changes. Dig around the root zone and see how dry the soil is. If it's dry, you need to water it.

• Observe the soil and notice how it feels when it has adequate moisture versus when it's dry and needs water. Notice how long it takes your soil to go from wet to dry. This will change as the summer season progresses, but once you know approximately how long it takes to dry out between waterings, you can apply the right amount at the right time. The key is getting water into the root zone and no farther.

• You can buy moisture sensors, or *tensiometers*, that indicate the soil's moisture level. Learning to use one can help you take readings at different spots in your yard. This is important because not all areas need water at the same time. Also, some sophisticated sprinkler systems have moisture sensors that control the different stations so they don't come on as scheduled if there's been a rainstorm.

• Determine how much water you need to apply to reach the root zone in your lawn or garden. For example, water an area of your lawn or garden with an inch of water. Wait about twenty-four hours, then dig down and see if water has penetrated to the root zone. If it has, you know how much to apply each time you water. If the root zone is still dry, repeat the experiment with two inches of water or until you get water into the root zone.

• Don't assume that all areas of your yard are the same. Run the above test in different spots to find out your yard's application rates. Different soils need water applied differently to soak down to the root level. Slopes may need slow soaking so water penetrates the soil rather than running off. Other spots may need only half as much water because the soil is better able to hold moisture.

• If you use a sprinkler system, set out small containers (tuna can size) and time how long it takes your system to fill the containers with an inch of water. Use this data to program your sprinkler system, or attach a timer to your faucet and hose.

Using the Right Type of Irrigation System for Your Location and Needs

There are many ways to get water to a plant's root zone. The system you choose should be based on your budget, local climate, time you can spend watering, and size of your yard and garden.

If you're putting in a new yard, you have an advantage in that you can integrate your irrigation system and landscaping with the latest technology. Some of the options you can choose from are:

• A great way to conserve water (up to 70 percent compared to sprinklers)and keep root zones moist is to install a drip system for your container plants or garden. A drip system has small diameter hoses with openings (emitters) that apply small amounts of water to each plant or container. A drip system can be a single line servicing a few containers or a high-tech whole yard system. In dry states like Arizona, a drip system reduces water loss from evaporation and makes a lot of sense, especially on hot, windy days.

• The hose and sprinkler system is easy, cheap, labor intensive, and inefficient. It's hard to rotate a sprinkler around a yard and get consistent coverage without wasting a lot of water. For small garden use, watering furrows with a hose can be effective. For lawns, it's not recommended.

• Underground sprinkler systems are the most popular way to water lawn and shrubs. The biggest advantage of these systems is that you can hook the lines up to a central timer and water during the night when evaporation loss is lowest. Because sprinkler systems are sensitive to water pressure, you have to design them carefully. A poorly designed system with too many heads or too wide a spacing won't deliver water where needed. In a new yard or when redoing an existing one, it's a good investment to hire a professional to design and install the system for uniform coverage and minimal water waste.

• A combination sprinkler and drip system gives you the best of both systems. Sprinklers can water lawn and shrubs while a drip system handles the garden, trees, and container plants. Consult a professional irrigation systems designer or equipment supplier for which will work best in your area and yard. A drip system will maintain trees and shrubs in good condition in the event of severe water restrictions. Lawns are much easier to replace than expensive trees and shrubs.

Capturing Water for Garden Use

Some dedicated gardeners believe city water has additives that are not good for their plants' health, so they capture and store rain and melt water.

In addition, storing runoff is also a great way to conserve water in times of drought.

There are several ways you can store water and use it in for gardens. One easy way is to place fifty gallon wood or plastic contains at the corners of the house. Water from the downspouts fills the containers whenever it rains. In fact, a 1,000-square-foot roof will easily fill four, fifty-gallon barrels during a one-inch rainstorm. That equals 200 gallons of water that can keep a garden going in a drought. Some homeowners go even further and install cisterns, or large buried containers, that can hold hundreds or even thousands of gallons.

If you're building a new home, you can optimize your landscaping to store water rather than let it run off. Walkways and driveways of crushed stone or gravel allow water to penetrate rather than run off.

Planting slopes to retain water so it soaks into the soil also helps. Check with local garden clubs and talk to homeowners who have installed these systems for ideas.

Recycling Water for Landscaping

When you're designing your new home's plumbing system, you can easily add alternate lines or valves to run used water from your washing machine, shower/tub drains, dishwasher, and bathroom sinks to a collection tank. If you mix this used, or gray, water with fresh water, it may supplement water for gardens and lawns. You could easily collect fifty to one hundred gallons of water a day.

However, there are several caveats to consider:

- You have to be careful which soaps, detergents, and bleaches remain in the water, so you may want to use only organic cleaning products. It's also best to recycle only the rinse cycles from the washer and dishwasher. Water from tubs and showers are usually no problem.

- You need to use the water from the collection tank the same day it is collected.

- Check your local codes before installing. Some codes don't allow recycling gray water.

- Contact your state department of environmental health for more information about what types of recycling are permitted in your area.

It's exciting to able to build your own home, incorporate the latest resource-saving technologies, and landscape according to your vision. Every home site is different and poses unique challenges and opportunities, but that's what makes it fun. When you trade ideas and experiences with other green homebuilders and join clubs with like-minded people, landscaping and gardening become never-ending adventures.

If you find that designing and building a new home is not the way for you, but remodeling an existing home is your vision of helping the environment, the next chapter will show you how.

PART 3

REMODELING TO MAKE YOUR HOME ECO-FRIENDLY

CHAPTER 7

PLANNING YOUR GREEN REMODEL AND WORKING WITH A GREEN ARCHITECT AND CONTRACTOR

Many homeowners are remodeling their current homes to be energy efficient, rather than buying a new green home. This makes a lot of sense. If you have a great location that can't be duplicated, want to add green features as your cash flow permits, and avoid big mortgage payments, remodeling can be a great way to go.

For first-time homeowners who can't afford a new green home, buying and remodeling a home is a good way to get started in homeownership. At the same time, they can help out the environment by adding eco-friendly features as they fix up the home.

Many homeowners who are considering remodeling express concern about stories they've heard that green improvements cost considerably more money. This is both true and false. If you look at green remodeling as an investment—putting money into the project and eventually receiving a return on that investment—green remodeling absolutely wins a thumbs up. While it's true that there are upfront costs in making eco-friendly improvements, such as installing solar panels, upgrading insulation, and replacing energy-leaking windows, you will recoup these costs over time in utility savings. How long that takes depends on your climate, your local utility rates, how high these rates climb in the future, and government credits or rebates.

For example, if you were to install a solar hot water system for $6,000 and receive $2,000 in rebates, your net cost would be $4,000. If you were to save $65 a month in water heating costs, it would take a little over five years to break even. And should utility rates go up (what are the chances of that?!) over the next few years, the payback time would shrink even more. Don't forget the intangibles, such as winter comfort levels due to passive solar windows, more energy independence with solar power, and the satisfaction of reducing your carbon footprint.

It's hard to come up with any compelling reasons *not* to remodel with green materials and techniques. You might point to the higher upfront costs as a possible negative, but government and utility company rebates are fast eliminating these speed bumps to making energy efficient upgrades the norm.

Although you may not be able to afford an award-winning green architect and build an energy efficient, one-of-a-kind dream home in an idyllic setting, this does not mean you're out of the game. You can still find an existing house and remodel it into an environmentally responsible home using recycled materials and the latest technology. It's not only exciting to create a home using your unique ideas, but a great investment as well.

Few aspects of real estate are more satisfying than remodeling an older home to make it better and more energy efficient. People who do this as a career provide a great service to the real estate market, recycling rundown houses and remodeling them into homes families can buy and live in for many years.

After you've finished your first green home, you may find that remodeling homes and renting or selling them is something you want to pursue. You'll know for sure when you say, "Wow, that was fun. Let's do it again." On the other hand, if it's, "Boy, I'm glad that's over; never again," don't worry about it; there are many other hobbies ... like golf or fly-fishing.

Some homeowners need only a month or two to design and remodel their homes from start to finish, while others find it's a work-in-progress that spans several years. Regardless of which way you go, the results are worth it. It's a great way to exercise and expand your creativity while becoming more energy independent.

To help you get started on the road to green remodeling, this chapter gives you plenty of useful tips on planning your project and finding and hiring the people you'll need to make it a success. In it you'll learn:

- How to finance your remodeling project

- How to plan your project, either on your own or with an architect

- How to find and work with a green contractor

- How to minimize your problems with complete and accurate paperwork

- How to deal with paying contractors and managing your costs

- How to handle the final walk-through and punch list

FINANCING YOUR GREEN REMODELING PROJECT

Most remodelers would agree that deciding what jobs should be tackled in what order can be downright intimidating, with a touch of panic mixed in. Where to start is the big question that probably scrolls across your mind. In reality, the scope of any remodeling project depends on how much money you have to spend, so that's where we will start.

Financing basics concerning how to buy a home and the nuts and bolts of green mortgages (EEMs) are detailed in chapter 1. However, when you own a home and need a source of funds to remodel it, your home's equity is the most obvious place to seek financing.

Mortgage lenders have recently tightened their credit requirements considerably, and credit scores along with loan amount-to-home's value (LTV) are prime considerations for how much you can borrow. Gone are the days when lenders would loan 125 percent of a home's value with a smile and a wink.

In mortgage-speak, the money you can borrow in addition to your current loan balance is called a *cash-out loan*. Most lenders will use the appraised home's value minus the current mortgage balance times x percent to determine your loan amount. For example, if your home appraises for $375,000 and you owe $260,000, you have $115,000 in equity. If the lender agrees to loan 70 percent of your equity, you get a cash-out loan of $80,500. At 80 percent, the loan amount jumps to $92,000 or at 90 percent to $103,500.

But there are trade-offs involved. Depending on the lender, your interest rate will likely increase as the LTV goes up. A loan based on 70 percent of equity will cost less than one at 90 percent.

The bottom line regarding how much you can borrow is that your interest rate and payments with a cash-out loan depend on:

- The value of your home based on a current appraisal

- Your credit score and verifiable income from tax returns or pay stubs

- The loan payments you qualify for based on your income

- The percent of your equity the lender is willing to lend

- The type of loan you're seeking, because not all loan programs require the same LTV

The most common sources of financing for homeowners who want to remodel include: *home equity lines of credit (HELOC)*, refinancing your mortgage, taking out a second mortgage, and borrowing against your IRA or other securities. As you might expect, each of these options comes with trade-offs, and you'll have to decide which option best fits your situation.

Before you commit to any kind of financing, talk to at least three lenders, get good faith estimates, and compare rates and terms. In addition, ask lenders if they have a green mortgage program (EEM) that allows them to lend slighter more money if the remodel incorporates energy-saving upgrades.

Home Equity Lines of Credit

HELOCs come in many variations. Some of the most common are:

- Loans with low or no up-front fees. One of the good things about HELOC programs is that when you qualify for a loan, no interest costs incur until you use the money. You pay interest only on the amount used.

- A choice of fixed or variable interest rates, which are the prime rate plus a percentage rate. You may also have the option to convert to a fixed rate. Be aware that some lenders push a teaser rate that changes in six months or a year.

- Programs that are typically five, ten, and fifteen years and can be amortized (you pay principal and interest), or the lender can require a minimum monthly interest payment.

- A loan of up to 90 percent of your equity or more, depending on your qualifying ratios

- Interest rates that can be less than a second mortgage or unsecured loan

- Interest rates are tax deductable for most taxpayers.

Refinancing Your Mortgage

The biggest refinancing disadvantage is that you pay steep closing costs. But if you plan to stay in the home for a few years and the new interest rate is lower than your present rate, it may be the best way to go. On the other hand, if you plan to sell in a couple of years, you're unlikely to recoup closing costs.

Four key questions you should ask yourself before refinancing are:

- Is the interest rate going to be at least one percent lower than your current rate?

- Are you going to stay in the home long enough to justify the high closing costs?

- Can you get more money by refinancing as opposed to any other cash-out options?

- Does the lender offer a green mortgage option when you make energy efficient upgrades? (See chapter 1 for details.)

Second Mortgages

If your existing mortgage has a great interest rate you don't want to give up, getting a second mortgage may be the most economical way to go.

For example, suppose your mortgage rate is 4.75 percent and the current rate to refinance is 6.15 percent. Increasing your mortgage rate 1.4 percent for thirty years and giving up a 4.75 percent loan may not be a good move. Instead of refinancing, you can leave your current mortgage intact and take out a second mortgage secured by your home. Many banks, credit unions, pension funds, insurance companies, and the like offer second loan programs. Like equity loans, interest on these loans is usually tax deductible.

Typically, lenders will lend 70 to 80 percent of equity on second mortgages, although some may go higher. The best strategy is to shop around for the best rate and terms.

Miscellaneous Sources of Remodeling Funds

Other often-overlooked sources of remodeling funds are loans against securities, savings accounts, pension funds, and insurance policies. Generous relatives should be considered, too.

One source worth checking out is a loan from your 401(k) plan. Typically, you can borrow up to 50 percent of your fund and pay it back monthly with an automatic payroll deduction. Some plans allow you to submit loan applications online; funds are often made available in a week or two. Check with your 401(k) provider, or read your plan's paperwork for details on how to apply, as well as to learn interest rates and payback terms.

When considering alternatives, remember that if you don't use your home as security, you may not be able to deduct any interest, so factor this into your tax planning. It may make a big difference in the overall cost of the loan.

Once you have loan approval and know how much money you have to work with, it's time to move on to the next step.

PLANNING YOUR GREEN PROJECT

If you're like most individuals who are considering remodeling their homes, your dream project starts out beyond what your budget allows. That means you have to do some triage and decide what's most important, what you can do now, and what you can do later. Deciding on trade-offs is never easy, especially when two or more people are involved in the decision making process. This is when you need a professional to help you sort out your options.

Finding a Green Architect

After securing financing, next you need to find a green architect to help you create your dream remodel. Yes, it's going to cost more, but the dividend is a remodel that fits your home's style and increases its value. The architect is also a source of expertise to help you shop for a green contractor and communicate your vision for your eco-friendly home.

So where do you find a green architect who shares your vision? Start by looking for remodeled homes with energy efficient upgrades. If you see one that you admire, ask the owners who did their design. It's likely these owners will be flattered and cooperative in giving referrals. This approach also applies to contractors, landscape designers, suppliers, and other building trades.

Other sources of information are green building publications and local environmental clubs, suppliers, and contractors who offer green building or remodeling. Once you've put together a list of architects, set up appointments for interviews. Afterwards, ask yourself the following questions:

- Does the architect listen to you and try to grasp your vision of what you want?

- Has he or she done other green remodeling jobs in the area? Where, and can you see them?

- Does he or she have a portfolio of green projects? Testimonials, awards, and memberships in professional organizations?

- Does he or she have a good working relationship with green contractors and suppliers in the area?

- Do you feel you can work with this person? Does it appear that you're on the same wavelength as you discuss ideas and ways to accomplish your dream remodel?

Handling Trade-Offs

After their credit union approved a $125,000 second mortgage on their 1979 ranch style home, Mark and Rachael set up a meeting with an architect they knew who specialized in green remodeling projects. It soon became apparent the homeowners' list of wants would need serious trimming. Upgrading the home's energy efficiency plus adding a bedroom and family room and enlarging the kitchen would put the costs way over budget. Clearly it was time to sharpen pencils.

Trimming a remodeling want list is rarely easy because the homeowner's emotions are often involved. In this case, Rachael had visions of her dream kitchen and Mark had visions of watching the Super Bowl in a spacious family room with a big screen TV. However, they both deeply cared for the environment, so the energy upgrades were a good starting point when deciding what to keep and what to delete from the list.

With the help of their architect, Mark and Rachael pared their list down by agreeing to give priority to the upgrades that reduced energy use. After the dust settled, here is how they determined their remodeling priorities.

Because their home had old aluminum single pane windows, upgrading to high efficiency windows topped the list. The double pane replacements would save considerable energy and take advantage of solar gain from their south-facing windows.

Insulating the walls and attic with cotton fiber and formaldehyde-free insulation came second on the couple's list. They wanted to insulate the attic to at least R-38 and the walls to R-12.

The 1979 gas forced-air furnace was down to about 50 percent efficiency, so that needed to be replaced with a new high efficiency vented model. They also needed to upgrade and seal the ducts.

With the home becoming nearly airtight, they decided to install a whole-house exhaust system with fresh air intakes, in addition to venting the range hood to the outside.

Replacing the old appliances with Energy Star-rated ones that could cut energy about 50 percent was important to Mark and Rachael as well, so that came next on their list.

The couple wanted to install solar power and hot water systems, but with the planned additions to the home, these would have to move to their deferred list. Instead, they opted for an on-demand water heater. The local power utility had a program that gave its customers an option to buy power generated from green sources for about five cents more per kilowatt-hour. Choosing that option would reduce their carbon footprint to the same degree as if they had installed their own solar generating system.

Also added to their deferred list was the half bath they wanted. Instead, the space became a closet, with accessible plumbing for adding the toilet and sink later on.

The 14-foot by 32-foot addition to the family room, enlarged kitchen, and a new bedroom used up about 90 percent of their budget. That left around $12,000 for unforeseen costs. However, rebates and credits from their energy-saving upgrades created some flexibility in the budget and made it possible for Rachel to get her concrete counters and kitchen island.

In the end, Mark and Rachael upgraded their home to an energy efficient, comfortable place to live. At the same time they reduced their energy use by more than 70 percent and increased the value of their home considerably.

Planning Tips and Traps

If planned upgrades increase the home's value significantly more than other homes in the area, sometimes it's best not to remodel, but to sell it instead and buy in a different area. Many remodelers try to make their home into something it isn't, creating problems down the road. For example, let's say you live in a neighborhood of 2,300-square-foot homes and need more room, so you decide to add on another 1,200 square feet. This could over-improve your home for the area; you wouldn't get the value out if you had to sell. It may be better to sell and buy a 3,500-square-foot home in an area of similar homes, then add the green upgrades.

Additional tips include:

• Create your own green remodeling dream team. Get together with your architect, builder, subcontractors, and other tradesmen for a planning meeting. It's critical that your remodeling plans and budget pass the reality tests: the builder and subs. Your architect has no way of knowing beforehand exactly what a builder will bid. For example, suppose you and the architect estimate that your project will cost $125,000. However, the builder notes that concrete costs increased last week, and the electrician points out that labor for installing solar panels and wiring is $1,800 low. After everyone has looked at the plans, added suggestions, and revised cost estimates, you find the actual costs are closer to $138,000. This gives you two options: scramble for additional funding or do some triage and cut costs. Many times, the team can come up with ways to cut costs without cutting items from your project. This can only happen if everyone is on the same page and there's good communication, though.

• Be aware that remodeling cost estimating is just that—estimating. Unforeseen problems, delays, and cost increases can put pressure on your budget. If possible, a 15 percent cushion over the bid amount is advisable. For instance, if your banker agrees to loan you $150,000 for the project, then keeping about $22,000 in reserve and striving to keep the bids around $128,000 gives you a cushion. And don't worry about having $22,000 left over at the end. You'll find good uses for it as the project progresses.

• If you plan to contribute sweat equity to reduce costs, the best time to bring it up with the contractor is your first meeting. Ask him or her to work up two prices, one including your sweat equity and one without.

Should you decide to go the sweat equity route, make sure you detail every-thing in writing. Note exactly what you plan to do, when you want to do it, and what dollar amount you are credited off the total cost.

• Be proactive about taking notes about meetings, changes, and any-thing else that you need to remember. It's too easy for the architect, builder, or you yourself to forget items discussed or changes that need to happen along the way.

• Budget-busting changes during construction are the biggest gators in the swamp. Make sure you have clinched the project the way you want it *before* construction begins. Making changes on paper is cheap, but dur-ing construction, that can get expensive fast.

• It's important to keep an open mind, stay flexible, and seek out ideas proactively when planning your project. It's likely the architect, builder, subs, or even suppliers have ideas they've picked up from other jobs that can make your project better and more efficient.

 Recommended resources that no remodeler should be without are:

Green Building Products. The GreenSpec® Guide to Residential Building Materials. Alex Wilson and Mark Peipkorn (New Society Publishers, 2005)

Green Remodeling, Changing the World One Room at a Time, David Johnston and Kim Master (New Society Publishers, 2004)

Fine Homebuilding Magazine, Taunton Press (www.finehomebuilding.com)

This Old House Magazine, www.thisoldhouse.com

Many homeowners have problems finding a good contractor because they don't follow through on the qualifying process. The next section gives you tips on how to improve your selection process.

FINDING AND WORKING WITH A GREEN CONTRACTOR

If you've found a great architect who shares your vision of a green remod-el, he or she may have worked and established a good working relation-ship with contractors he or she can recommend. Ideally, you should talk to and get bids from at least three contractors. The process for creating your short list is similar to the one for finding a green architect. For instance:

- Look for other homeowners who have remodeled their homes and get referrals.

- Ask local tradespeople, suppliers, real estate agents, and people active in the green or environmental community for referrals.

- Keep your eye open for remodeling jobs in progress. Contractors often plant their signs on lawns or in windows of jobs they're working on. When you see one, stop and talk to the homeowner.

- Sometimes professional organizations or clubs hold open houses of recently upgraded green homes. Understandably, these owners are proud of their homes and welcome a chance to share ideas and referrals.

- Look for remodeling contractors who are members of the National Association of Home Builders (NAHB—www.nahb.org/local_ association_search_form.aspx) or the National Association of the Remodeling Industry (NARI—www.nari.org/search/chapters). Both Web sites feature green remodeling tips you can download, as well as listing members in your area.

An excellent Web site is www.buildinggreen.com, if you live in an area that has few builders, if you're qualified to do the work yourself, or if you simply want green building information. This site offers a number of informative green building publications and a wealth of green product specs.

Shopping Tips for Finding a Contractor

Admittedly, interviewing and checking out contractors is tedious work. However, sketching out your remodeling ideas on a legal pad and turning a contractor loose with them is risky, and you may not like the results. To improve your chances of getting the green remodel you want at a price you can afford, don't shortcut the hiring process. Follow these ten tips to improve your chances of making a good choice:

1. If a contractor on your short list doesn't return your call, show up on time for the initial meeting without calling to let you know he'll be late, or doesn't show up at all, cross that person off your list fast. If a con-

tractor isn't reliable and doesn't respect his or her clients' time, it's unlikely you'll have a good working relationship.

2. Check out one of the contractor's job sites. If it's organized and efficient, count that as a big plus.

3. It's also a plus if the contractor belongs to professional organizations such as the NARI. Members must attend a training class to qualify as an NARI-certified green remodeler.

4. The contractor should be willing to give you copies of insurance paperwork verifying liability and workers' comp, as well as a copy of his or her current contractor's license.

5. If the contractor offers you the addresses of previous jobs and testimonials from past clients, add this to the plus column. Consider it an even bigger plus if the contractor arranges for you to see a couple of past jobs.

6. It's important that the contractor be willing to work closely with your architect and others involved in your project. If the contractor has a hard-to-get-along-with reputation, cross him or her off your list.

7. Put a check in the plus column if the contractor listens to you and respects your ideas but offers suggestions for better ways to get the job done or save you money. After all, it's experience and know-how that you're hiring.

8. Check the local Better Business Bureau and the state agency that oversees contractors for complaints. You may find a few, because it's almost impossible to work in highly emotional situations such as remodeling without encountering impossible-to-please hotheads. What's important is how these complaints were resolved and how fast.

9. Put another check in the column if the contractor uses a professionally written construction contract and has no objection if you want your attorney to look at it. Before you sign any contractor's contract, make sure you understand it thoroughly.

10. The last thing you want is for subcontractors to come back to you for unpaid work or suppliers for unpaid invoices. Ask the contractor for a credit report and list of suppliers who extend him or her credit. It's common to read about contractors who don't pay their subs or suppliers, and after the job is completed, these unpaid parties record liens against the property. It's a good idea to follow up toward the end of the project with the subs and suppliers and make sure they have been paid.

If you know an excellent contractor, but he or she hasn't had any green remodeling experience, should you still hire him? Because in many areas of the country there are few experienced green contractors, this happens quite often. After meeting with the contractor, ask yourself the following questions:

- How willing is the contractor to try new things and make sure his or her subs follow the plans?

- Do you have a green architect who can work closely with the contractor?

- How knowledgeable are you and can you work with the contractor to make sure the job goes the way you want?

An excellent contractor should have no problem installing most of the green upgrades you need. It may take more time for some of the subs to learn to work with unfamiliar products, but it can work out. Good resources are www.greenhomeguide.org/guide_for_green_renovation/index.htmlis and guidelines from the Earth Advantage green building certification program (www.earthadvantage.com).

Using Earth Advantage or LEED guidelines, you can remodel a home incorporating green materials and techniques. A good contractor who is willing to learn and follow these guidelines can be a good choice.

Deciding on Which Bid to Accept

You may think that choosing among competing bids is going to be like computing a moon-shot trajectory, but they're seldom grouped that close. Here are a few tips that'll help you through the process:

- Low bids are not likely to be top quality or the best choice. Perhaps the estimator missed something, or the contractor will end up coming back for more money to complete the project. Be suspicious of any bids that are substantially lower than the rest.

- The highest bid isn't a guarantee of good work or necessarily the best choice either. Some builders submit high bids when they don't want the job; it's a good way to say no without offending anyone. Others may not be competitive for one reason or another.

- Most often, bids in the middle are more realistic and are the ones you should focus on.

What If There Are Few Contractors in Your Area?

In small towns and rural areas, there may not be contractors experienced in green remodeling. This doesn't mean you can't install energy-saving upgrades and complete a green remodel. However, you'll need to do some homework and become familiar with green remodeling techniques. *The LEED for Homes Reference Guide* is a good resource and is available at www.usgbc.org/Store/PublicationsList.aspx?CMSPageID=1518.

When Greg and Teva decided to remodel their 1960s one-level frame home in a rural Idaho town, they wanted to make it energy efficient. Unfortunately, there were no contractors in that area, and the nearest home improvement centers were seventy miles away. However, the homeowners did a lot of homework on green remodeling and energy efficiency and knew a couple of good carpenters.

Because their propane heating bill was a big budget item in winter, they felt passive solar and solar panels for hot water would pay for themselves in just a few years. Factoring in federal and state energy incentives, the return was especially attractive.

Fortunately, Greg and Teva's home faced south, so installing low E windows would collect considerable solar gain in the winter. Unfortunately, the existing front windows were smaller than the owners wanted, so it took considerable carpentry work to enlarge the openings. With the new, larger low E double pane front windows installed, solar gain dramatically increased.

To further trap solar heat, the owners replaced their old nylon carpeting and installed dark tile and wood floors. As it happened, they knew a stone mason who lived nearby and hired him to rebuild and enlarge the old fireplace using a local igneous rock to provide a heat absorbing mass.

For heating, the remodelers decided on a solar hot water system that heated water for both domestic use and radiant floor heating. For cloudy days with little solar gain, they would also need to add a propane boiler as backup.

Greg and Teva needed skilled help to install the solar systems, and a supplier in Boise helped them line up a heating, ventilation, air conditioning (HVAC) contractor who had experience with solar systems. Because it was a seventy-mile one-way trip for the installers, the homeowners had to have the prep work ready so the installs could be completed in one day. Otherwise, a return trip for the install crew would add hundreds of dollars to the bill.

Other projects the owners were able to do on their own included adding wall and attic insulation and installing Energy Star appliances and water-saving fixtures. Next year, they hope to install solar power and reduce their power bill to as close to zero as possible.

The next important aspect of your remodeling project is the paperwork. Complete and accurate contracts, addendums, schedules, change orders, and so on make the project go more smoothly.

MINIMIZING PROBLEMS WITH COMPLETE AND ACCURATE PAPERWORK

Before any work begins on your remodel, everything should be in writing and signed by all parties involved. Incomplete paperwork is responsible for more lawsuits, glitches, misunderstandings, lost time, and extra costs than all other problems combined. It's a good idea to keep in mind that old real estate adage: If it isn't in writing, it doesn't exist.

All parties should sign and date the original contract and any extensions, change orders, and addendums. Additions to the contract that happen as the project progresses, such as addendums and change orders, are numbered 1/x.

A good contract spells everything out clearly. Ask yourself the following questions:

- Does the contract have a start and end date? There may also be completion dates for certain phases of the project.

- Who is responsible for obtaining the building permits and paying the fees? Usually the builder gets all the permits needed and bills you. Sometimes the fees are part of the bid.

- Who will supervise the subcontractors, handle problems, and be the boots-on-the-project to make sure everyone is on the same page?

- Does the contract spell out how the contractor protects the house from construction dust and debris? It should be specific, such as using six-ml plastic sheeting or tarps supported by a framework enclosing the work area.

- How are change orders handled? What happens if you see something that looked great on paper but doesn't look as great as the project takes shape? What are the costs and penalties?

- Does the builder include a warranty? What does it include and how long is it good for?

- Does the contract have a provision for binding arbitration if there are misunderstandings that both parties cannot resolve?

- Are there attachments or addendums that detail the work and materials used? For example, a contract that says: "Tear out old deck, dispose of debris, and build new twelve-foot by fourteen-foot deck" is too vague. A better one would read, "Remove old deck, dispose of debris, and install new footings, posts, and handrails. Decking to be two-inch by six-inch cedar, custom knotty grade, finished with two coats of Sherwin Williams DeckScapes semi-transparent, medium-oak stain. Work and materials to be in compliance with all local building codes and agreed upon green practices."

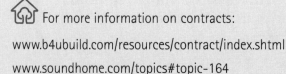 For more information on contracts:

www.b4ubuild.com/resources/contract/index.shtml

www.soundhome.com/topics#topic-164

www.abcaforms.com/education5.html

www.hometips.com/articles/pros_permits_safety/contract_types.html

www.diyonline.com/servlet/GIB_BaseT/diylib_article.html?session.docid=91

PAYING THE CONTRACTOR AND MANAGING YOUR COSTS

It's not always easy handling the money side of a remodeling project. Both you and the contractor are probably wary of getting burned, so it's important to work out a payment plan you're both happy with. Some common approaches are cost-plus or time-and-materials, fixed-fee agreement, and capped cost-plus.

Cost-Plus or Time-and-Materials

Cost-plus or time-and-materials specifies that you pay for all the materials and the contractors are paid an hourly fee in addition to a 15 to 35 percent markup for their overhead and profit. The final bill lists hours worked and paid material invoices. Contractors like this approach because it guarantees them a profit. You tend to get good work, but have to stay on top of the project because costs can easily go over budget.

Fixed-Fee Agreement

With a fixed-fee agreement, you usually eliminate surprises at the end. There's usually a mutually agreed-upon allowance for unforeseen changes—$1,000, for example—and everything over this you pay for at the time of the change. In new construction, these are called change orders, and clients typically pay up-front for any added changes or extras.

From the contractor's side, if he can complete the job for less than the bid, his profit goes up. But on the flip side, unforeseen problems or sloppy bid-work may result in little or no profit.

A plus to this approach is that you know what the costs are up-front, with no surprises. However, if a contractor underbids or runs into problems, he may rush the job or cut corners to save money. This is why you should be wary of bids that are significantly lower than the others.

Capped Cost-Plus

Capped cost-plus hybrids combine features from cost-plus and fixed-fee agreements. For example, you can cap a cost-plus contract with a guaranteed maximum price. If costs stay under the max, you save money; if costs run over, the contractor pays the difference.

The trade-off is that you get the savings, which means that the contractor has no incentive to cut costs. However, you can increase incentive by offering to split the savings. To reap the maximum from this plan, you need to stay on top of the project.

Other Ways of Managing Your Costs

There are other ways of managing your costs as well. These include the following tips:

- Never pay for the whole job up-front. Begin with no more than 10 percent to get started. Have spaced payments tied to benchmarks, such as insulation completed, solar water heater installed, all windows installed, and radiant floor heating completed.

- Hold the final 10 to 15 percent until the final inspection is completed and any problems are corrected to your satisfaction.

- Schedule an early meeting with the contractor each day. It's important for you and/or your architect to stay on top of the project. Also, have an end-of-workweek meeting to make sure everything is on schedule and within budget.

- Avoid letting a disagreement become confrontational. You may have to go the extra mile to maintain your cool, but it's worth it. That a roofer accidentally drops tar on your new Lexus is not license to lose your cool. True, you need to be firm and make sure the contractor keeps his or her promises as per the contract, but letting a disagreement dissolve into a confrontation can sabotage your project and add to your costs.

- Don't second-guess your contractor. Asking third parties their opinion of the job can cause problems. Often there's more than one way to do a job, and getting conflicting opinions just muddies the water. Stay the course you've committed to unless there's good reason to believe a problem exists. Good communication between you and your contactor usually prevents unwarranted misgivings that end up costing you money.

HANDLING THE FINAL WALK-THROUGH AND PUNCH LIST

No matter how smooth the first 95 percent of a project goes, the last 5 percent carries the most emotional weight. It's likely the contractor is in the process of moving on to his or her next job, and you just want your job wrapped up so you can live in a construction-free zone.

The key to the final phase is to schedule a walk-through with the contractor so you can work up *a punch list*—a list of things that need correcting: wall dings, leaks in the solar water heating pipes, a failed seal in a double pane window that allows it to fog up, and a bathroom exhaust fan that doesn't work.

Before the Final Walk-Through

An important part of completing a project is the final walk-through, when you and the contractor go over the job and make sure it's to your satisfaction. If problems are found, you and the contractor work up a punch list of what needs correcting.

Depending on the job size and your contract, you should still owe the contractor 15 to 25 percent, to be paid upon completion of the walk-through or the punch list.

The following tips will help smooth out the walk-through:

- Review your contract; make sure you have copies of all change orders and addendums.

- Make a checklist of products you need to get paperwork for, such as warranty paperwork on windows, solar panels, boilers, appliances, and so on.

- Walk through the jobsite and jot down anything that needs finishing, problems you see, or questions you may have.

- If you don't trust your expertise, hire a home or energy inspector to walk through with you.

- Make sure the site is clean and construction debris is being recycled as per your instructions.

- Get at least half a gallon of each paint used, with labels showing mixing formulas.

 More info on punch lists:

www.servicemagic.com/rfs/toolbox/docs/punch_list.doc

www.ownerbuilder.com/punch-list.shtml

www.bxmagazine.com/article.asp?ID=87

The Punch List

Ideally, when you walk through the project and create a punch list, it should include these five things:

- It should be a multi-part form so that all parties get a copy.

- It should list all the problems that need correcting. Remember: If it isn't in writing, it doesn't exist.

- A dollar value should be assigned to each item on the list. Later on, if you have to escrow funds to ensure completion, this gives you the amount.

- Each item's completion should have a deadline.

- Both homeowners and contractor should sign and get copies upon the walk-through's completion.

If you've stayed on top of the project and solved problems along the way, your punch list should be short. But suppose everything checks out except for a solar panel that was damaged during installation. In this case, you might want to hold out one-and-a-half to two times the panel's cost. This gives the contractor or sub the incentive to follow through or allows you enough funds to have it done by someone else.

A long, messy punch list is often the result of not reviewing each day's work, not communicating regularly with the contractor, or letting problems slide until the end. Certainly you don't want to be a pest on the job, but a quick inspection with the contractor at the end of each day or phase yields big dividends at the end.

Now that you've got a good idea of what planning and working with an architect and contractor entails, the next chapter looks at green materials and remodeling tips for your home's interior.

CHAPTER 8

REMODELING YOUR HOME'S EXTERIOR WITH ECO-FRIENDLY MATERIALS

Whether you're remodeling your present home or a home you have recently purchased, difficult decisions on what to upgrade first are the norm, especially since funds are often tight and you must triage carefully. Chapter 7 recommended that upgrades that reduce energy use and monthly utility bills go to the top of your list. Replacing the ugly vinyl kitchen floor or countertop can wait. While this is true most of time, there are important exceptions. When your home isn't water-tight and winter approaches, your priority may quickly become making your home's envelope weather-tight—which is the subject of this chapter. In it you'll learn:

- How to make your roof eco-friendly
- How to replace your siding with eco-friendly materials
- How to upgrade to energy efficient windows
- What your options are with eco-friendly stains and paints
- What materials to use to build an eco-friendly deck, patio, or fence
- How to recycle and dispose of construction waste

MAKING YOUR ROOF ECO-FRIENDLY

If your roof needs to be replaced, consider using green roofing materials. These are not only eco-friendly, but when you factor in longevity are in line cost-wise compared with standard roofing.

Traditional roofing materials, like asphalt shingles and rolled roofing, are toxic not only to you but the environment as well. These petroleum-based products give off a host of toxic gases, especially when heated by a hot summer sun. These gases can then enter the house through open windows and doors. To compound the problem, when you replace the roof, all this material goes to a landfill or incinerator that adds more toxins to the environment.

Unfortunately, some homeowners and landlords take the short-term view and go with the least expensive roofing materials, usually twenty-year asphalt shingles. While this may be the least expensive way to go up-front, it may not be the case over the long term. Other roofing options can provide double the lifespan and quality for only about 50 percent more investment. Even if you're planning to sell your home in the near future, selecting quality eco-friendly roofing materials can increase the value of your home and make it more saleable.

In one case, a homeowner preparing his home for sale replaced an aging asphalt shingle roof with recycled metal panels. These panels featured a durable baked-on finish that made the home not only attractive but able to quickly shed snow after a heavy storm. The roof also had a lifetime warranty that boosted the home's selling features. Although the home market was slow, the home sold for full price in just a few days. At closing, the buyers admitted that the roof was a major reason they made an offer. So many homes they had looked at previously had problem roofs or roofs that would need replacing in a few years.

If you have just acquired your home, you may have a recent inspection or roofing report that estimates the number of years before the roof will likely need to be replaced. However, if you've lived in your home for a while and know the roof is more than ten years old, you should consider getting an inspection, especially if it's constructed of asphalt shingle, flat rubber membrane, or tar and gravel.

The purpose of the shingles is to cover and protect the tarpaper or plastic water barrier that covers the plywood decking. This barrier prevents water from soaking through the plywood deck, which can cause a long list of expensive problems to your home's interior.

Aging tar and gravel roofs with a low pitch are good candidates for sheet metal roof replacement. If there's no slope, then a layer of polystyrene insulation over a waterproof membrane is a more environmentally friendly replacement than asphalt. For these types of roofs, you can also apply waterproof coatings. When shopping, look for low volatile organic compounds (VOC) emissions, recycled materials, and reflective surfaces to reduce heat gain.

For a flat roof, adding a layer of soil over a waterproof membrane and turning it into a green living roof is an interesting concept. Plant drought-tolerant, low-growing plants for a unique eco-roof.

An ignored leak that starts out as a cheap fix can easily escalate into a credit card-maxing repair bill. In one case, a homeowner ignored a spreading brown stain on the ceiling above the kitchen dining area. One evening, as the family was setting the table, the ceiling above it suddenly gave way and chunks of sheetrock crashed down. Luckily no one was hurt, but they had to find another place to live fast, and the owner faced a sizable repair job.

As soon as the stain appeared, the homeowner should have looked for the source or called a roofing contractor. Lesson learned from this is to be vigilant and look for leaks regularly. It's critical to catch problems early, before the repair bill balloons.

One trap you want to avoid is assuming that because you have twenty-year asphalt shingles (or even the more expensive thirty-year architectural shingles), you won't need to re-roof for twenty years or more. In reality, the durability of the shingles depends on variables such as climate, the quality of the installation, and whether the shingles have southern or northern exposure, or both. Shingles on some twenty-year roofs with extreme exposure can degrade in seven to twelve years and need replacing sooner than anticipated.

Prevent ice dam damage to your roof. When snowmelt runs down the roof, it can pool behind ice that has frozen in the rain gutters and created a dam. As this water pools, it backs up under the shingles onto the decking. If it penetrates the decking, it can leak into insulation and flow along rafters to drip many feet from the entry point. Damage can be extensive, especially if mold develops. To prevent ice dams, insulate the attic walls and ceiling so rising heat cannot melt snow on the roof. Also, install a waterproof barrier between the decking and the shingles.

To get an idea of your roof's condition, check the shingles from the ground with binoculars. Look for:

- Shiny or bare spots where the mineral coating has worn off

- Curling or degrading corners

- Broken or missing shingles

- Flashing around pipes, chimneys, or vents that is cracking, discolored, or deteriorating

- Valleys where two sides make a V, which are natural drainage channels and can take a beating from snow and rain

- Edge shingles that have been lifted or damaged by ice dams over the winter

If you find some of these problems, you may need to consider a new roof. The first step is to find a roofer who is familiar with green roofing options, and then decide which material is your best choice considering trade-offs and budget.

Finding a Quality Roofer

Sometimes finding a good roofer is not easy. Locating someone who is knowledgeable about green roofing options may take some time. If choices are limited, you'll need to do some homework and find out what green roofing materials are best for your local area, and then find an experienced roofer who is willing and able to install the type of green roof you want. You may have to talk to several until you find one you feel can do the job. An experienced roofer willing to try something new can usually figure out and complete a successful install.

Shopping tips for finding a good roofing contractor include:

- Ask for referrals from people who have recently hired a roofing contractor.

- Check with general contractors (especially those who do green building) you know for recommendations.

- Ask architects, suppliers, and others who are involved in green building for referrals.

- Interview and get bids from at least three experienced roofing contractors.

- Explain up-front that the bid should include recycling the tear-off debris so it doesn't end up in the landfill. You may get some raised eyebrows on this and have to hunt around on your own for a facility that can recycle old shingles and tar paper. You don't want this stuff to end up in the landfill if avoidable.

Taking Advantage of Green Roofing Options

The initial investment in some green roofing products may cost a little more than traditional petroleum-based products. But when you factor in the life span, green roofing becomes a strong competitor; add in the environmental costs, and it's no contest.

There are a number of options to choose from. If your remodeling budget is tight and you must scrutinize every dollar spent, consider installing recycled asphalt shingles. Although these products contain recycled asphalt, they also use waste paper and other recycled materials. Life expectancy is about the same as traditional asphalt products. Be sure to use the lightest color roofing materials you can find, because the more solar radiation that reflects off the roof, the cooler the attic and home are on hot summer days.

Other green roofing choices to consider:

- Fiber-cement shingles are an environmentally friendly choice. Made from Portland cement, sand, clay, and wood fibers, shingles are Class A fire-rated and typically come with a fifty-year warranty. Available in different textures and colors, this option makes an attractive roof. Again, go with the lightest color possible to minimize summer heat gain.

- Metal roofing made of aluminum, copper, or steel is a popular choice for homeowners because it can last fifty years or more. It works well on low- or steep-pitched roofs, and in heavy snow areas it solves the problem of ice dams. When made from recycled metals, it's an environmentally friendly way to go. Panels, shakes, tiles, and shingles are available. If you live in a fire risk and/or high wind area, metal can be an especially good choice. One minor drawback is that you need to use similar metals for roofing, flashings, and fasteners. If dissimilar metals used for the roof and the fastener get wet, a weak electrical current is created that can corrode metal.

- Plastic shingles are durable, and some manufacturers warrant their products for fifty years. They can look like slate, tile, or regular shingles and come in different colors. These products can be recycled so they don't have to end up as landfill. Some are recycled rubber tires mixed with binders and green additives. They do a great job mimicking slate tiles and cedar shingles, and they are fire resistant. The initial cost of these products is usually slightly higher, but when you get fifty to seventy-five years from a roof, this can be a bargain.

• Slate and clay tile roofs are natural products, both recyclable and environmentally friendly. However, if you need to ship the heavy tiles long distances, you lose a lot of the eco-friendly gain. You may want to check for companies that sell recycled tiles. Typically, these roofs last a hundred years or more, are attractive, and add to a home's value. The biggest disadvantages are the high initial cost (almost double that of shingles) and weight. You may also have to reinforce the roof framing before installing these types of roofing.

Insulating and Weatherproofing Your Roof

In addition to the protective layer of singles or other material, two other important components that add to your roof's effectiveness are insulation and a waterproof covering.

If you have to tear off the roof's plywood decking and replace it, choosing SIPs is a good energy-saving choice. *SIPs, or structural insulated panels,* are like a sandwich with *oriented strand boards (OSB)* and expanded polystyrene insulation as the filling. OSB consists of wood scraps glued together into a panel similar to plywood. You can buy SIPs with a variety of insulation cores and skin materials. A big plus is that they're strong, precisely cut, and won't shrink or warp from temperature or humidity changes the way traditional wood does.

It's important to note that not all SIPs are alike; some manufacturers make greener products than others. To choose an eco-friendly manufacturer:

1. Look for one that is located as close as possible to you to reduce shipping.

2. Make sure the manufacturer uses non-formaldehyde adhesives, such as a non-toxic soy-based glue.

3. Look for non-toxic insulation foams, such as polyisocyanurate.

4. Look for *Forest Stewardship Council (FSC)*-certified wood content. This ensures you aren't buying old growth or non-sustainable wood products.

If your roofing contractor is not familiar with SIPs, contact the Structural Insulated Panel Association (www.sips.org) for a list of workshops near you. These workshops for contractors and homeowners focus on how to use SIPs. You can also find a list of certified installers around the country.

After you've torn the old shingles off and found that the decking is in good condition, with no leaks, you'll likely need to only replace the underlayment, which is a waterproof layer between the decking and the shingles. PVC sheeting, polypropylene, or asphalt-saturated felt paper is commonly used. However, PVC and asphalt-based paper aren't environmentally friendly, so you may want to check out sheeting made of polypropylene or recycled tire rubber.

Using Flashing to Prevent Water Damage

Pipes, vents, and chimneys that extend through the roof should have flashing—metal, plastic, or rubber material that seals openings—to prevent water from using them as a route into the attic. Other areas, such as roof valleys and eaves, also need metal or plastic flashing to provide extra protection.

Metal step flashing protects the joints between the roof and dormer walls and chimneys. It fits to each course of shingles and looks as if it is stepping up a wall or other surface.

Valley flashing protects the valleys where two roof planes meet. This W-shaped channel goes over the top of the protective deck covering before the shingles or other roofing materials are installed. Vent pipe flashing fits over flues and pipes. They are typically cone-shaped, with a flange at the base. Other types are rubber or synthetic materials that create a seal where the vents exit the roof.

Drip-edge flashing is strips of plastic or rubber that run along the roof's eaves and rakes to prevent water from seeping under the roofing when backed up by ice dams.

When you inspect your roof, look closely at the different flashings for any corrosion or deterioration and replace if needed. Flashing failure can allow water to enter the house and cause mold and other budget-busting damage.

After roofs, siding often shows up as must-do before winter winds blow. Green replacement siding options is the next section's focus.

REPLACING YOUR SIDING WITH ECO-FRIENDLY MATERIALS

If you're remodeling your home's exterior, some environmentally friendly materials are available that combine good looks with fifty-year-plus warranties. Replacing your siding gives you an opportunity to upgrade your house warp and insulation at the same time. Because many older homes don't have well-insulated walls or moisture barriers, they have high utility bills and are susceptible to mold growth from water infiltration.

Insulating Your Walls

After you've torn the old siding off your home, you'll want insulate the walls before installing a vapor barrier/house wrap and new siding.

There are several retrofit green insulation options available. These include:

- Paper-faced fiberglass or recycled cotton batts between the studs, which create a good thermal barrier

- Cellulose made from recycled paper that is blown into wall cavities

- Sprayed-in foam, which forms a good air barrier and insulation, but is more expensive than other options

Finding a good insulation contractor is about as important as the product. Installed correctly, insulation makes your home environment comfortable and protects your investment. Incorrectly installed, it can max out your credit card from repairing rot and mold after water infiltrates the insulation.

To find an experienced insulation installer, follow the steps on hiring tradesmen and contractors outlined in chapter 4 and consult the next section.

Protecting Your Home with Housewrap

When your old siding is removed, you'll likely see asphalt-coated paper nailed or stapled to the studs, although some homes may have plywood sheathing under the paper. It's important to install an air and moisture barrier before the siding goes on to make your home air- and water-tight.

Whether you're upgrading existing siding or adding a new wing, there are several green options that can insulate and protect the home against heat loss and water infiltration, including the following:

• A slightly more expensive but energy efficient approach is to install structural insulated panels (SIPs). As previously discussed, these panels are a sandwich of two layers of oriented strand boards (OSB) with a rigid foam core filing. After the SIP panels are attached to the studs, a waterproof layer of fifteen-pound builders felt, or housewrap, is installed on the outside face to protect the panel before the siding goes on. Because these panels are pre-cut at the factory and come ready to install, it's important to find a contractor who is familiar with SIPS and their installation. Most homeowners who install SIPs recoup the extra cost within a few years from lower utility costs.

• Driving around new homes under construction, you've likely seen homes sheathed in a pink wrap or silver one with Tyvek printed in bold letters. This and other similar housewraps serve three purposes:

1. They create a weather barrier behind the siding, preventing water from getting through.

2. They prevent air from infiltrating the home and reduce heating and cooling costs.

3. They allow moisture within framing or insulation to escape to avoid rot or mold growth.

• Some builders still prefer to use fifteen-pound felt paper that creates a good water barrier and absorbs moisture. Which product is best usually boils down to what the builder has found to be successful in his experience and in your area.

• There are dozens of effective housewraps on the market. Some are designed for specific types of siding applications. Others do a good job across a broad spectrum, such as Tyvek, which has about 70 percent of the market.

• Like SIP panels and insulation, installing housewrap requires an experienced contractor who knows and has experience installing the product. A good installer not only overlaps the material's seams, but also tapes them to ensure an airtight install. A bad installer often shortcuts this process, and that can cause problems later on.

Informative housewrap Web sites:

www.tyvek.com

www.pinkwrap.com

www.typarhousewrap.com

www.covalencecoatedproducts.com

www.green-guard.com

Making Use of Green Siding Options

Once the water and air barriers are in place, the next step is installing the siding itself. There are more green options than ever before to create an attractive home with great curb appeal. Some good options come from using recycled products found at salvage yards, building teardowns, or demolition sales. For example:

• Cedar shingles not only make a good roof, but good siding as well. You can use reclaimed shingles for either trim or full siding.

• Aluminum siding is a good product, often replaced by vinyl or PVC in recent years because they are cheaper and easier to install. Unfortunately, vinyl siding is not an environmentally friendly material and is difficult to recycle, so you should avoid using it.

• Wood lap siding in good condition can be given a second life if it's sanded and primed on both sides before the face side is painted or stained.

• Used brick can make an attractive exterior, although removing the old mortar can be labor-intensive. If you get it cheap or free, the cost of cleanup can be worth it.

According to *Consumer Reports,* siding contractors generate more complaints to Better Business Bureaus than any other trade. To protect yourself, ask for proof of licensing, get at least three bids, be wary of the lowest one, and get references and check them out. Referrals from contractors and architects are the best sources.

The biggest problem with wood siding is that it needs a protective coat of stain or paint every few years to increase its longevity. To overcome this and to save a few trees, there are some new green siding products on the market that last fifty years or more and create great curb appeal.

One excellent eco-friendly product is fiber-cement siding. It's made from cement, sand, and cellulose fibers and is available in planks or panels. It can mimic wood lap siding and, in sheet form, looks like stucco or wood paneling.

Fiber-cement siding won't warp, melt, burn, or attract termites, and it inhibits fungal growth. You can paint it, it's easy to install, and it's a good choice in fire areas. It may also reduce your insurance costs.

Stucco is another good siding product. Made primarily from cement, sand, and water, it creates a attractive, durable, fire-resistant siding. Different manufacturers include additives in their product that make it easier to install, resist cracking, and create attractive textures.

However, if you own or are thinking of buying a home sided with synthetic stucco, or *EIFS (Exterior Insulation Finish Systems)*, that was popular a few years ago, you may want to get a professional stucco inspection to make sure there isn't water damage behind the siding.

EIFS is a synthetic material that resembles real stucco, but it isn't a cement-based product. Synthetic stucco, installed on an insulated sheathing board with fiberglass mesh, produced a good siding economically. But problems from careless and inexperienced installers allowed water to infiltrate and rot the wood framing behind the stucco.

High-profile lawsuits and news media attention gave EIFS products a bad name and created problems for some owners who wanted to sell their homes. Due to potential water infiltration problems, be sure to make your offer on an EIFS-clad home subject to a professional inspection. If there are nasty surprises behind the siding, you can still back out of the deal and get your deposit back.

After siding and roofs, no remodeling job is complete without upgrading to energy efficient windows. The next section helps you decide which options are best for your green remodeling project.

UPGRADING TO ENERGY EFFICIENT WINDOWS

There are several options available for upgrading your windows to more energy efficient models. Whatever option you choose, make sure the windows are at least Energy Star-rated and that you obtain NFRC (National Fenestration Rating Council—www.nfrc.org) ratings based on your climate and use.

The most common ways to upgrade windows follow.

- If the window frame is in good condition, you can replace only the window and sash. This is usually the most economical way to go. However, it's important to make sure the window frame is square and the replacement is a snug fit and won't leak.

- You can replace both the frame and sash with complete window units that fit into existing jambs. It makes the window unit more bulky because of the added window frame, but it's the easiest way to upgrade.

- The most expensive and best option is to replace the entire window unit along with new flashings and sealants. Since you've removed everything and are starting with a framed opening, you can easily enlarge or change its dimensions to fit a different size window. This gives you an opportunity to enlarge south-facing windows to get the maximum solar gain.

Like most other remodeling products, window quality is often a function of cost. But in the real world, the difference between lower-cost vinyl frames and the more expensive aluminum is sometimes hard to measure. Choices are often made based on style, looks, and architectural compatibility.

There are also intangibles to consider, such as manufacturer and warranty. A small local company may make great windows cheaper than a major national company such as Pella or Marvin, but will that company be around in ten years? If a double pane window loses its seal and fogs up, will the warranty cover it? Typically, a top-of-the-line window manufacturer will warrant a double pane seal for twenty years and the frame for ten years. Also, be wary of lifetime warranties. "Lifetime" often boils down to how long the company stays in business.

The four most popular replacements are:

1. Vinyl, which is a popular choice because it doesn't corrode, is low maintenance, and is usually less expensive than other options. When you shop around, focus on the manufacturer's reputation and warranty. A bargain window isn't a good deal if it fogs up between panes or leaks air and water. Colors are usually limited to white or beige.

2. Wood windows, which are attractive and come primed from the factory. You can paint them to blend or contrast with the home's exterior. With good maintenance (meaning that you need to paint every few years), wood windows can last a long time. Typically, they are more expensive than vinyl windows.

3. Fiberglass, which is more expensive than wood or vinyl but is also more durable and maintenance free. You can paint fiberglass to match your décor. It is less bulky than other options and makes a good choice for large-view windows.

4. Aluminum-clad windows, which are the most expensive (about 30 percent or more expensive than vinyl), but are durable, low maintenance, and have a slim profile. Manufacturers offer a large palette of colors and can even custom-match colors to fit your décor.

The bottom line on buying windows is that you can't tell how good a window is by looking at it. You need to factor in the manufacturer's reputation and how long they've been in business, and you need to read the warranty's fine print.

After deciding what window type fits your budget and décor, the next thing to focus on is the glazing.

To be energy efficient, the glass will be double or triple paned, depending on your climate. In northern climates, you want all the solar gain you can get in the winter; but in the South and Southwest, windows need to block heat gain. Within the same house, glazing can also vary from south-facing windows to those on the north side.

The key to making good window choices is to start by reading the National Fenestration Rating Council (NFRC) sticker attached to most new windows. Chapter 5 details how to read the glazing information on these stickers. However, it's worth repeating here the details on three important numbers found on NFRC stickers:

1. U-Factor represents conductive heat loss through the window. Look for 0.35 or less; a smaller number reflects better energy efficiency.

2. Solar Heat Gain Coefficient, or SHGC, is a measure of the amount of solar radiant heat that passes through the window. In hot climates, you want a low SHGC number (0.35 or less) to reduce your cooling costs. For cold climates, look for 0.50 or higher, because you want all the heat gain you can get on those sunny but chilly Arctic Express days.

3. Low-E coatings are nearly transparent metal or metallic oxide films. They allow visible light to pass through but reflect much of the long-wavelength radiant energy. This is great for summer and hot climates, but for cold winter locations you'll need to shop for low-E (or no E) coating with high SHGC glazing to allow as much solar energy as possible to pass through. Depending on your area, you may have to special order high-value SHGC glazing with no E coating. The downside of high SHGC glazing is that in summer you'll need to install reflective blinds or screens to counter the heat passing through these windows. Planting deciduous trees for summer shade and adding extended eves can also help control solar gain.

When your roof, siding, and windows are weather-tight and energy efficient, you can turn your attention to less critical but still important tasks, such as staining or painting house trim, sheds, fences, decks, and so on. Exterior paints and stains can be highly toxic, so it's important to find eco-friendly products. The next section tells you how.

USING ECO-FRIENDLY STAINS AND PAINTS

According to the Environmental Protection Agency (EPA), stains, paints, and other architectural coatings produce about 9 percent of the *volatile organic compound (VOC)* emissions from consumer and commercial products. VOCs are carbon compounds that evaporate at room temperature and react in sunlight to form ground-level ozone. They also can cause respiratory, skin, and eye irritation, headaches, and other problems to homeowners applying high VOC products.

Even though some products have low VOCs, they are produced with toxic chemicals that come from nonrenewable resources and are energy-intensive or polluting to manufacture. This means you'll need to do some homework before you buy.

Reducing VOCs in paints and stains and making them more environmentally safe is an ongoing project for most major paint manufacturers. Going with good quality products from major manufacturers such as Sherwin-Williams, Dutch Boy, Pittsburg Paints, Benjamin Moore, Pratt & Lambert and others is a good start. They have low VOC and eco-friendly product lines that give good results. Avoid unknown brands and unlabeled and discount bulk paints.

Selecting Green Stains and Sealers

House trim, fences, sheds, decks, and other wood structures need regular maintenance to protect them from water and sunlight degradation. Some homeowners prefer stains—clear or pigmented—to keep these structures looking good, then they brush on sealers or coatings that protect wood from the elements. You can also get products that combine both in one application.

Typically, three types of wood stains and sealers are available:

1. Natural oil stains made from linseed, tung, and soya oil come from renewable resources and can be a good eco-friendly choice. Few people are allergic to them, and they are long lasting and don't require a sealer. A possible downside is that clean-up requires high VOC solvents.

2. Acrylic/urethane products have good water resistance, but their manufacture is polluting and energy intensive. Clean-up requires high VOC solvents. These products are not a good eco-friendly choice. A better choice would be water-based stains and sealers.

3. Water-based stains are probably the best green choice. They have low VOC content, clean up with water, and involve fewer toxic products in their manufacture. Look for stains that have no glycol ethers. Because water-based stains are slightly less durable than acrylic/urethane products, you may want to apply a water-based sealer as a protective top coat.

Choosing Green Paints

Not all wood surfaces are protected with stains. Some applications, such as siding, fascia, and soffits, are better protected with exterior paints. Like stains and sealers, you want to find products that have low or zero VOCs and are not energy-intensive or polluting to make.

Just about all major paint manufacturers offer lines of low or zero VOC paints. However, you may not be able to find the paint you need in one of these lines, so it's important to read the labels and know what you're applying.

Paint contains three major components: Pigment that gives it color, a binder, and a solvent to keep the mix in liquid form until you apply it. Two common types of paint are latex and oil-based. Latex uses water as a solvent, while oil-based paints use a petroleum-base. But just because latex paints are water-based doesn't necessarily make them environmentally friendly. Binders and pigments also determine how green paint is.

Latex paints have lower VOCs than oil-based products, can be recycled, and are good for exterior applications. Look for 100 percent acrylic paint with a 30 percent or more solids content. You'll find this information on the can's label. Typically, better paint quality means a higher price. However, good quality paint looks better, lasts longer, and goes on easier than a cheap product. In the long run, buying a top-of-the-line paint is more economical.

Oil-based or alkyd paints use binders derived from petrochemicals. In some exterior applications, they give better coverage than latex paints and are toxic to mold and mildew. Some professional painters prefer these paints for exterior use, but for homeowners who don't want to keep the toxic solvents needed for clean up around, it's best to stay with latex products.

When buying paint, look for suppliers where the professional painters go rather than mass-market outlets. If you pull into a paint store and the parking lot has several painters' vans with ladders on top, you've found the right place. These shops have knowledgeable people who can answer questions and direct you to the right product for your application.

Staining and painting outdoor wood structures gets old fast, and there are products that make this unnecessary. The next section looks at the best of these replacement alternatives.

For more information on green paints and stains, go to:

www.greenhomeguide.com/index.php/product/C229

www.greenplanetpaints.com

www.ecowise.com/index.php?cPath=21_97_222

www.ecoindia.com/products/paints.html

www.sherwin-williams.com/pro/green/index.jsp

www.benjaminmoore.com

BUILDING AN ECO-FRIENDLY DECK, PATIO, OR FENCE

Decks, patios, and fences are primarily wood structures that traditionally came from non-sustainable sources. They also used toxic stains and wood treatments to slow down rot and insect damage. Fortunately, there are alternative replacement products that last longer and are more environmentally and homeowner friendly, and you won't have to use toxic chemicals to preserve the wood every year or so.

Adding a Deck Using Green Materials

Adding a deck is a popular home improvement for many owners. It not only increases backyard enjoyment, but also adds value to the home. *Remodeling* magazine's 2007 "Cost vs. Value" report estimated that when a home sells, an owner recoups 85 percent of the deck's cost.

Traditionally, homeowners favored building decks from redwood, Western red cedar, pressure-treated Southern pine, or imported exotic woods. These woods all make attractive decks, but come at a high ecological cost. However, there are now alternative decking materials that are eco-friendly and maintenance free.

Two popular choices are plastics and composites. Plastic decking is made of eco-friendly vinyl, and composites are composed of 50 to 60 percent wood fiber and polyethylene. These products have many advantages over wood. For example:

- Both composites and vinyl decking are recyclable.

- They don't need toxic chemical treatments every year or so.

- They conserve natural resources.

- This deck is more dimensionally consistent, resulting in less waste.

- Insects don't find these products gourmet friendly.

- You can sit out on your deck without guilt over destroying prime cedar or redwood.

Rather than use non-renewable woods for decks, consider these alternatives:

www.fpl.fs.fed.us

www.certainteed.com

www.doityourself.com/stry/nonwood

www.ideas-for-deck-designs.com/vinyl_decks.html

www.trex.com/

www.askthebuilder.com/551_Composite_Decking.shtml

Constructing a Patio as an Alternative to a Deck

Constructing a patio is an alternative to building an expensive deck and allocates resources more effectively. When built out of bricks or local stone, patios are durable, maintenance free, and attractive. Materials are low cost and often free of charge. One homeowner's neighbor gave him the flagstone from his patio when he tore it out to construct a wood deck. Three years later, the deck-building neighbor was complaining of the high cost of maintaining the deck on top of the initial investment.

Patios constructed from bricks, stone, or cast concrete pavers on a sand bed are an excellent way to go for the do-it-yourselfer. They are not only eco-friendly, but allow water to percolate through rather than run off. You can build this type of patio to be as simple or elaborate as your time and budget allow.

Rather than build a wood deck, construct a green patio. Check out these patio building Web sites:

www.landscaping.about.com/cs/hardscapefences1/ht/brick_patio.htm

www.pavetech.com/guides/bpatio.shtm

www.popularmechanics.com/home_journal/gardening/2827546.html

www.rd.com/18277/article.html

www.askthebuilder.com/Patio.shtml

Building a Fence with Green Products

As they did for decks, homeowners often used lumber from non-sustainable trees for fences. Now many alternative fencing products are eco-friendly and derived from sustainable sources, such as bamboo, vinyl or plastic, composite, cinderblock, local rocks, and recycled wood.

One homeowner who had a rusted chain link fence along one side of his house didn't like the idea of digging out concrete-anchored pipe fence posts to remove it, so he planted several Virginia creeper vines along its length. About eighteen months later, green foliage covered the fence. In the fall, the foliage turned an attractive red, and what had been an eyesore became a landscaping plus.

The lesson learned is to look for ways to recycle eyesore fences into something attractive with plants. The slats may be at the end of their life-cycle, but if the posts are in good condition, you can install wire or mesh between them and plant vines or other creeping plants. Other green alternatives to fences are hedges and closely spaced bushes.

Another homeowner rebuilt his fence from recycled wood he got free from a farmer tearing down an old barn. Look for sources of wood for outdoor structures from houses, factories, and other structures slated for demolition.

Replacing siding, re-roofing, remodeling, and adding on to your home creates a lot of waste and debris that should be recycled and disposed of in an environmentally responsible way. Next are suggestions on how to do that.

RECYCLING AND DISPOSING OF CONSTRUCTION WASTE

As a homeowner concerned with the environment, you likely know how important it is to recycle and minimize waste going to the landfill. Because remodeling and new construction produces so much waste, it's a good idea to make plans to dispose of it in an eco-friendly manner. If you wait until construction debris is several feet deep in your front yard before thinking of how to dispose of it, your stress level will soar.

For example, a typical kitchen remodel can easily produce between twenty and thirty cubic yards of C&D (construction and demolition) waste and fill a twenty-two-foot-long by eight-foot-wide by six-foot-deep roll-off dumpster. Fortunately, not all this has to go to the landfill. With prior planning, you can recycle it, give it away, or use it in your remodel and save on dumpster rental and landfill fees.

Recycling and reusing material from your remodel is limited only by your imagination. Some suggestions include:

- Instead of thinking "demo," think "deconstruction:" taking care to tear out old construction for the purpose of reusing or recycling it. For instance, two by fours are reusable, as are old kitchen counters and cupboards, which can find new life in the garage or workshop. Call local salvage yards and find out what materials they prefer and sort accordingly.

- Intact windows, flooring material, counters, sinks, light fixtures, and so on can go to salvage yards, be sold at a garage sale, and be advertised in a local paper as free "you haul."

- You can sell or give metal products to recyclers. Even old water heaters, furnaces, and air conditioners are valuable for their recyclable metals.

- Lumber is reusable if you tear it out with care.

- You can get rid of working appliances at a yard sale, set them on the curb with a "free" sign, or donate to a local charity or second hand store.

CHAPTER 9

REMODELING YOUR HOME'S INTERIOR WITH ECO-FRIENDLY SYSTEMS AND MATERIALS

When remodeling your home to make it environmentally friendly, it's common to have more projects in mind than funds to see them through. This means having to triage: which improvements do you have the time and/or money to make now and which can be put off for a while? Often, the projects that are delayed are those you really want to do—such as replacing the yellow counter tops, the avocado range or refrigerator, or the 1980s vinyl flooring you can't stand—but are not priorities toward making your home more ecologically sound.

Eventually the time comes when you've completed your exterior projects and the home's shell is water-tight and energy efficient. Now you can focus on the projects inside your home that make home ownership fun. Today is a great time to upgrade, because there's an abundance of green products on the market that promise to make your home's environment safer and more comfortable than ever before. In addition, new energy efficient appliances and materials offer unlimited opportunities to express your creativity. Mix and match is the new wave in interior decorating. Stodgy conformity and granite countertops are passé. To give you an overview of how to make your home's interior more eco-friendly, as well as one you can be proud to show off, this chapter will cover numerous options in green upgrading. In it you'll learn:

- How to create a ventilation system that consistently replaces air throughout the house

- How to upgrade your heating and cooling systems to make them energy efficient

- What to choose and use in eco-friendly stains and paints

- What options are available in environmentally friendly floor coverings

- What appliances and materials can be used to create a green kitchen

- How to upgrade your bathrooms with eco-friendly fixtures and materials

VENTILATING YOUR ENERGY EFFICIENT HOME

When you wrap a house in air- and waterproof materials and insulate it so that no cold or warm air escapes, it's going to be energy efficient. But it's also going to be like living in a plastic bag. Some of the negative consequences of tight building wraps are:

- Indoor air pollution can build up to the point where the house becomes toxic.

- Humidity increases to the condensation point and creates ideal conditions for mold and fungi growth. To monitor the relative humidity level, you will need a *hygrometer,* or moisture meter. Relative humidity readings above 50 percent mean you need to install dehumidifiers to prevent mold from becoming a problem. For more information on hygrometers, check out www.indoorhealthproducts.com/humidity-sensors-buying.htm

- Commonly used products such as paint, cosmetics, hair spray, cleaning products, and so on give off gasses that contaminate inside air.

- Building products that use formaldehyde glues, synthetic carpets, or oil-based painted surfaces give off toxic gasses called VOCs, or volatile organic compounds.

- Biological contaminants from pets, dust, and microscopic critters can accumulate and cause allergic reactions or asthma.

- Cooking is a big source of VOCs that contaminate inside air.

The top interior project for your "to do" list is ensuring the home doesn't become toxic from indoor air pollution. To prevent your newly remodeled home from becoming a sick house, you need to create a ventilation system that consistently replaces air throughout the house.

Designing a Whole House Ventilation System

Older homes replaced air through many leaks and loose fitting components, but they also lost a lot of energy in the exchange. With the new energy efficient building standards, indoor air quality has to balance heating and air condition with bringing in outside air.

There are several ways to do this. The best approach is to hire an HVAC (heat, ventilation, air conditioning) professional to design a ventilation system to fit your remodel. Ideally, the furnace, AC, and whole house exhaust fans should work together, so you'll want to incorporate professional expertise in the initial planning. If you're using an architect or design/build team, ventilation will likely be included.

Typically, whole house vent systems incorporate a *heat-recovery ventilator (HRV)* to minimize venting the warm air that heats your home to the outside. In hot climates, you would install an *energy-recovery ventilator (ERV)* that reduces venting the cool air you've paid for.

Of course, as the ventilation system releases air to the outside, fresh air needs come in to replace it. The heat exchanger in the HRV tempers the incoming cold air with the vented warm to reduce energy waste.

 Ventilation Web sites:

www.sheltersupply.com

www.hvi.org/consumers.html

www.eere.energy.gov/consumer/your_home/insulation_airsealing/index.cfm/mytopic=11860

www.pathnet.org/sp.asp?id=7280

www.resourcecenter.pnl.gov/cocoon/morf/ResourceCenter/article//1467

Minimizing Humidity in Hot and Humid Climates

Hot and humid climates can present special challenges: You can't open windows and let the moist air out or turn on a fan to bring drier air into the home. Humid outside air added to interior moisture-laden air from dishwashers, cooking, showering, and so on can create even bigger problems. Steps need to be taken to minimize humidity inside the house. Suggestions on how to achieve this are:

- Install hardwood floors rather than carpet

- For walls, choose brick, tile, or plaster and avoid drywall

- Install a dedicated dehumidifier as part of your ventilation system

Installing Ventilation Systems in Other Areas of Your Home

Cooking emits high levels of VOCs and odors into your home's air supply, and if not vented, pollutants can cause problems. Many homeowners have installed unvented range hoods that use filters. Unfortunately, these are ineffective at removing VOCs and odors, so it's better not to use them. Hoods that vent to the outside through either the roof or a wall are more effective.

For effective venting, most kitchens require a hood that moves at least 200 cubic feet of air per minute (cfm) or five air exchanges per hour.

Bathrooms, being smaller, should have a fan vented to the outside that can remove at least fifty cfm. Look for low noise fans that you can wire into a separate timer switch that will shut the fan off in ten to fifteen minutes.

> Not venting your bathroom or neglecting to use the existing bathroom vent are major causes of peeling paint, curling wallpaper, mold, and wood rot. If family members often forget to turn the fan on during showers, consider wiring the light and fan on the same switch. Or to save energy, replace the on/off switch with a timer switch for both lights and fan. Look for a switch that allows you to adjust the timer.

Fan noise is an important consideration as well. Without getting into the physics and psychology of sound, you'll want to buy a bathroom or kitchen hood fan that operates with less than three sones. (A sone is a unit of sound measurement). Fans that run continuously, such as attic fans, should emit one sone or less.

When shopping for a hood, look for an Energy Star rating, 200 cfm or larger fan size, and a low sone rating (three or less). Also, look for lighting options that provide the amount of light you want over the stovetop. Check out www.thisoldhouse.com/toh/article/0,,220906,00.html for more hood information.

If you have an attached garage, you may want to install a fan to vent car exhaust to the outside. Fumes from driving your car into or out of a garage can easily seep into the house and add dangerous pollutants to the interior environment. Adding a timer to the fan switch so the fan continues running ten to fifteen minutes after you shut the garage door will effectively vent the space.

Ideally, venting should integrate with your heating and cooling systems. Again, to achieve the most healthful and energy efficient interior, hire a professional to help plan your remodel and integrate the HVAC systems.

UPGRADING YOUR HEATING AND COOLING SYSTEMS TO MAKE THEM ENERGY EFFICIENT

Among the most important energy-saving upgrades you can make in remodeling your home is upgrading the furnace and air conditioning. In colder areas, the cost of heating the home is easily 60 percent of the yearly utility bills. Adding a high-efficiency furnace to a home with housewrap and upgraded insulation can dramatically decrease heating/cooling costs.

Considering Green Heating Options

If you have a natural gas, oil, or propane forced-air system with ducts, you have several options to cut costs and increase efficiency:

- You can upgrade an older furnace to a new high-efficiency Energy Star model. If you've already upgraded your insulation and housewrap, you may be able to go with a smaller furnace and cut costs. Depending on the climate, monthly heating savings should pay for the system in about eight years or less.

- By taking advantage of passive solar gain with south-facing windows and heat-absorbing floors, rock or concrete walls, and other inside structures, furnace use and size can be reduced even further.

- You can tie a whole house ventilation system into your ductwork. Adding the incoming and outgoing air vents discussed previously can provide a constant supply of fresh air to your home.

- A filtration system can filter the air to reduce airborne particles that cause allergies and asthma.

- You can add humidifiers in dry climates and dehumidifiers in humid areas to increase your home's comfort level.

If you don't have existing ductwork or you need to heat an addition, *hydronic radiant heating* can be a good way to go. This type of heating uses a boiler to heat water that circulates through radiators located throughout the house or through tubing laid under the floors. Advantages of hydronic heating are:

- You can install a solar water heating system with a small boiler backup for cold, socked-in days.

- Many homeowners prefer these systems because of their constant and even heat.

- Installation is easy because there's no ductwork to install. Radiators are typically low profile units mounted along baseboards. Radiant floor heating uses no ducts or radiators.

- Radiant heating is dust-free because there's no circulating air to carry dust, pet dander, or other particles.

- There's a cost savings because you're not wasting energy heating air in the ducts and rooms.

- With radiant heating, you heat only those rooms you want to heat.

- For heating small areas, the water heater can provide the hot water.

Another energy efficient and green heating system is a geothermal (ground-source or water-source) heat pump. The system collects heat from the ground or a pond and cycles it through a compressor.

In geothermal systems, polyethylene pipe is buried horizontally four to six feet deep or in a vertically drilled shaft 100 to 400 feet deep. The pipes are filled with antifreeze or water that cycle through the heat pump. The pump extracts heat in the winter and reverses in the summer for cooling. These heat pumps are more expensive to install than other systems, but with their high efficiency, the investment break-even point can be as little as five years.

When shopping for geothermal heat pumps, look for an Energy Star-rated system and compare the costs with other systems to see which is best for your house and climate. Advantages of geothermal heat pumps are:

- Excess heat from the heat pump's compressor transfers to the hot water tank, reducing the cost of heating water.

- Heat pumps are quieter and smaller than conventional forced air systems.

- You can use existing ducts for a retrofit system.

- Energy costs can be up to 44 percent less than electrical heating systems, according to EPA data.

- Maintenance costs are low due to fewer exposed and moving parts.

For more geothermal heat pump information:

www.geoexchange.org

www.igshpa.okstate.edu

www1.eere.energy.gov/geothermal

www.epa.gov/energystar

www.homeblue.com/heating-cooling-1-geothermal.htm

When considering a new HVAC system, it's important to size the unit to your climate and house dimensions. Many homes have systems over-sized for the square footage that waste energy and money. The best way to determine if your system fits your house size is to have a heating contractor or energy auditor run a *Manual J heat loss analysis*. This procedure, published by the Air Conditioning Contractors of America (ACCA), calculates the amount of mechanical heating and cooling required for a building. Manual J enables contractors to estimate heating and air conditioning loads more accurately. Using Manual J, a contractor calculates heat loss from the building through walls, ceilings, and leaky ductwork, as well as heat gain from sunlight, people, lights, appliances, and so on. Your system shouldn't rate more than 25 percent over the peak hourly demand.

It's also important to check your furnace's ductwork for leaks, which can reduce efficiency up to 20 percent. Look for taped seams that may be leaking and re-tape. After remodeling, remember to have a professional duct cleaner clean the system to remove dust and debris. You may want to clean the duct system every couple of years thereafter. A buildup of microorganisms in the ductwork can make a house toxic.

Replacing Your Water Heater

If your water heater is more than eight years old (look for a sticker on the side for manufacture date), you may want to consider upgrading it. Popular options are:

- Replace the unit with a new more energy efficient water heater. New models have more insulation and are more efficient. This is often the most economical short-term route, if you're watching costs.

- Solar water heating systems are gaining in popularity. They are more expensive initially, but over the long term, you'll save about 90 percent of the cost of heating water. A good option is to install a solar system that services both domestic hot water and radiant heating through either radiators or floor tubing. You would need a small boiler/tank or tankless heater for cloudy days, but the long-term savings can be considerable.

- Tankless water systems are growing in popularity. Tubing circulates water through a heat exchanger that doesn't activate until you turn on a faucet. It's more energy efficient than keeping a tank of water heated. A tankless system can also be part of a solar system for even more energy savings. Typically, tankless systems last twice as long and cost half as much to use as a tank water heater.

- If you're heating your home with electricity, a heat pump system is more efficient than a conventional electric water heater.

More information on water heating:

www.aceee.org/consumerguide/waterheating.htm

www.home.howstuffworks.com/water-heater.htm

www.tanklesswaterheaterguide.com/

www.energystar.gov/ia/new_homes/features/WaterHtrs_062906.pdf

www.energyright.com/waterheat/index.htm

Upgrading or Installing an Energy Efficient Fireplace

It's no secret that fireplaces are highly inefficient and exhaust warm air and pollutants to the outside. However, they are cultural icons for many home-owners, who feel that not having one would take away from the home-owner experience. In addition, fireplaces add value and are a sales feature. A few ways to have a cheerful fire and minimize the negatives include:

- Upgrading a wood burning stove or a fireplace insert to burn pellets. This will significantly reduce pollution. Pellets are small cylinders of compressed sawdust that burn cleaner than wood. The stoves and inserts have controls that balance air and fuel for more efficient combustion. Look for products that are EPA certified.

- Install a natural gas log. Burning gas eliminates creosote buildup in the fireplace's chimney and having to dispose of ashes.

- If you live in an area with abundant wood, upgrade to an EPA-certified wood burning stove or insert. These units use outside air for combustion, which reduces creating negative air pressure in the home.

When the need for a cheery fire passes and summer heat takes over, thoughts turn to staying cool. Suggestions on how to do that are next.

Reducing Your Air Conditioner Usage

A central air conditioning unit is probably the biggest energy user in your home. To find out what it's costing you, pick a utility bill for a month your AC isn't running; then take the bill from the hottest month, when your AC was heavily used. Subtract the two months' power bills, and the difference is a good estimate of your monthly AC cost. For many homeowners, it's not unusual to spend close to $1,000 a year in cooling costs.

If you're in the remodeling or design process, consider the following to keep your AC's cooling load as low as possible:

- Upgrade your housewrap and insulation before sizing the cooling system. A well-insulated home will not need as big a cooling unit as one that hasn't been upgraded.

- High performance low-E, argon-filled windows will reduce the cooling load by more than half.

- Wide roof eves (24 inches or more) will shade the windows from the summer sun.

- Install radiant barriers on the underside of the roof rafters and insulate the attic and ductwork.

- Install a programmable thermostat that shuts off the AC when you're not home.

If you're planning to install a newer more efficient AC, preferably, Energy Star-rated, you'll want to make sure it's the right size for your home. The biggest AC replacement problems are:

- The AC salesperson sells you a unit too big for your home and square footage.

- The refrigerant levels and airflow are not optimal.

- Ductwork is poorly designed and installed.

Unfortunately, many contractors feel that bigger is better, but it's you that's paying the bill, so insist on Manual J sizing that takes into account especially hot days. If a contractor or salesperson uses a rule-of-thumb method or your home's square footage to estimate AC size, shop elsewhere.

Finding a Competent HVAC Contractor/Installer

Finding a good contractor or installer isn't always easy, so it's important to do some homework and get at least three bids. Ask the following questions before you commit:

- Ask if the intended installer has completed any training programs.

Several certification programs are available through the *National Association of Training Excellence* (NATE – www.natex.org) Also, major manufacturers offer training and/or certification on their HVAC systems.

- Ask if they use Manual J for sizing AC systems to the recommended house size and temperature for your climate. Also, make sure the evaporator and condenser coils match.

- Ask if they seal the ducts, test the system for leaks to 10 percent or less, and test airflow at the evaporator coil.

- Ask the oldie but goodie questions: Can they provide references and do they have complaints filed with the state and Better Business Bureau.

For more AC information check out: www.greenseal.org/certification/standards/residential-ac-central.cfm.

Once your AC system has been installed, you then face the challenge of lowering your usage. There are a number of things you can do to accomplish this, including:

- Open windows and run fans at night to cool the house down as much as possible.

- Keep windows closed in the day and circulate cool interior air with ceiling fans.

- Install reflective blinds to reduce solar gain.

- Close off unused rooms.

- Reduce the use of heat-generating appliances on hot days.

- Reduce inside humidity by venting the bathroom after showering.

- Make sure the clothes dryer vents to the outside and not the attic or garage.

- Run the dishwasher and clothes washer and dryer in the evening.

- Replace your furnace/AC system filters monthly.

- Plant deciduous trees that can shade the home in the afternoons.

Once mechanical systems are installed and working, remodelers' thoughts often turn to the fun stuff—color and decorating. Suggestions on how to make that safe and green are next.

CHOOSING AND USING ECO-FRIENDLY STAINS AND PAINTS

A big reason many people want to buy a home is so they can decorate the way they want without incurring the wrath of their landlord or jeopardizing their deposit. Of course, if you already own your home, or have just bought one, this is not a concern. Nevertheless, there's a deep inner need for us to personalize our space with color, and off-white walls just don't cut it. So whether you're thinking about making changes to your present home or are looking forward to redoing the home you've recently purchased, there are a wealth of options to consider.

Now is an exciting time to remodel or redecorate. New products are continuously appearing on the markets that are not only environmentally friendly, but attractive as well. Interior stains and paints have been significantly improved by manufacturers in the past few years to reduce low volatile organic compounds, or VOC formulations, that can be toxic.

Stains and paints give off the highest concentrations of VOCs during application and until the coatings dry. To keep your home as free of them as possible, consider these tips:

- Buy low or zero VOC paints and stains.

- Pick a time to paint or stain when you can open windows and create airflow throughout the house long enough to allow the trim and at least two coats to dry.

- Cover soft furniture such as couches, chairs, and beds, as well as other fabrics that may absorb paint and stain fumes, in plastic.

- Clean up rollers and brushes outside to minimize VOCs inside the home.

It's important to buy stains and paints through reputable manufacturers. Major suppliers such as Sherwin-Williams, Dutch Boy, Pratt & Lambert, and others have low or zero VOC water-based paint and stain lines. Many cheap and imported coatings contain high levels of toxic ingredients not listed on the labels. It's better to avoid any paint or company that you can't hop on the Web and check out.

Top-of-the-line paints and stains cost more but are easier to use, have low VOCs, and last longer. In the end, it's more economical to go with the best quality product. This also applies to brushes and rollers; top quality makes your paint go on easier and look better.

Good painting and stains Web sites to check out:

http://www.greenplanetpaints.com/

http://www.sherwin-williams.com/pro/green/greensmart_designation/

http://www.ehow.com/how_2107229_buy-nontoxic-interior-paint.html

http://www.thegreenguide.com/doc/96/paint

http://www.doityourself.com/scat/interior

Along with personalizing a home with colorful walls, floor coverings are at the top of many homeowners' decorating list. Fortunately, there are many eco-friendly options, and manufacturers are starting to get the message and produce more green products.

SELECTING ECO-FRIENDLY FLOOR COVERINGS

Floor coverings have typically not been eco-friendly. Carpets and padding give off toxic gasses, wood floors come from non-sustainable trees, and vinyl (PVC) flooring is toxic. As a result, you need to be more cautious and do some homework to find green floor coverings.

It's important while shopping around to match flooring to climate. For example, carpeting in hot and humid areas may not be as good a choice as wood or tile flooring. In colder climates, carpet and padding may add a layer of insulation over a cold floor.

Whatever your flooring tastes are, this section will point out shopping tips and buying traps to avoid.

Shopping for Environmentally Friendly Carpeting

The bad news is that carpeting, which accounts for 70 percent of flooring choices in the United States, is associated with health and environmental problems. That means many people are exposed to toxins that shouldn't be. Carpet padding or backing is also toxic and contains approximately 200 different harmful chemicals. In addition, most used carpeting and padding isn't recyclable and won't biodegrade. According to EPA figures, landfills acquired over 2.5 million tons of discarded floor coverings in one year.

The good news is that more manufacturers are marketing environmentally friendly carpets and padding. Still, you have to cut through the hype to make sure you buy what the ads promise. The key to finding eco-friendly carpeting is to read labels, ask lots of questions, and check out the manufacturer.

Consider these carpet-shopping tips:

- Look for carpets made from recycled materials.

- Read the labels to make sure no toxic materials are included during manufacture.

- Check out natural fibers such as wool. However, most imported wool carpets have a pesticide coating on the fibers.

- Nylon requires high energy to produce, and its production involves carcinogens and all sorts of VOCs you don't want in your house. In other words, it's a material you want to avoid. Instead, consider polyester *(polyethylene terephthalate—PET)*. This is a fiber usually manufactured from recycled plastic packaging such as soft drink bottles. It's not as durable as nylon, but it works well in light or medium traffic areas such as bedrooms.

- Look for third party labels, such as GreenSeal.

- Padding can also be toxic, so look for products made from recycled or natural fibers, such as jute.

The bottom line on carpet is to use it sparingly. There are greener and more durable products available.

Choosing Between Vinyl Flooring and Linoleum

While popular and economical, vinyl flooring is not recommended as replacement flooring because it's made from toxic PVC and is often glued in place with adhesives that are also toxic.

A good substitute is natural linoleum flooring, which is made from linseed oil and cork. Popular years ago, it was replaced by cheaper vinyl, but is now making a comeback due to the aforementioned environmental concerns regarding vinyl. Manufacturers are introducing new colors and patterns, and linoleum is available in both sheets and square tiles.

For more information on linoleum:

www.armstrong.com/resflram/na/linoleum/en/us

www.healthyhomeplans.com/articles/information8.php

www.thisoldhouse.com/toh/article/0,,202857,00.html

www.linoleumstore.com/

www.greenfloors.com/HP_Linoleum_Index.htm

Consider Tile for Your Floor Covering

Tile is an excellent choice for floors; it's durable and eco-friendly, especially when produced locally. It's available in several sizes and styles and can incorporate recycled materials such as glass and crushed rock. Easy to install and economical, tile is great for do-it-yourself projects. In fact, many home improvement centers offer free install classes and will rent out tile cutters. When you contribute the labor, it's easy to install a durable tile floor for less than two dollars a square foot.

If you have a south-facing room with big windows, large heavy tiles make an excellent floor choice, because they store heat and slowly release it after sundown. Tiles are also good choices for kitchen and bath floors, as well as countertops and backsplashes.

What's more, decorative recycled glass tiles are becoming popular as kitchen and bathroom backsplashes.

Informative tile Web sites:

www.lowes.com/lowes/lkn?action=howTo&p=BuyGuide/ChooseFloorTile

www.thetiledoctor.com/repair/floorremoval.cfm

www.doityourself.com/scat/ceramic

www.ceramic-tile-floor.info/index.htm

www.hometips.com/content/tile_intro.html

Contemplating Wood or Laminate Flooring

Wood flooring can be an environmentally friendly way to go, provided the wood comes from a sustainable source. Look for Forest Stewardship Council (FSC)-certified wood. The FSC is a non-profit organization that promotes responsible forest management. When you buy wood products with FSC certification, you know the product comes from a sustainable source. However, the stains and finishes applied to wood floors can be toxic, so it's important to use water-based and low VOC products.

The upside of wood flooring is that there many varieties available, and you can install a beautiful floor with inlays and different wood patterns. The downsides of hardwood floors are that they are pricey, not very durable, and require routine maintenance and care. Even the most recent technological advancements in surface treatment have not been able to solve such problems as scratching, fading, denting, and staining. If you've ever had a black Lab (or equally lovable canine) run across your wood floors, you've learned firsthand that wood flooring isn't that durable.

One homeowner with wood flooring and two Labs replaced the wood with laminated flooring; three years later, it still looks good. With its machine-made construction and hardwood photographic laminated surface, it's the perfect solution, offering the look and appeal of real hardwood while being more economical and durable, as well as easier to maintain.

If you're determined to stick with wood flooring, one sustainable wood is cork. Made from the outer bark of the cork oak tree, it's harvested sustainably without killing the tree. It's durable, sound absorbing, and naturally moisture-, rot- and mold-resistant. When shopping for cork flooring, avoid urea-formaldehyde binders and instead look for polyurethane or all-natural protein binders. Also, avoid cork-PVC laminate tiles and those with a PVC top coat.

Bamboo, a fast-growing tropical grass that's sustainable and durable, is another floor material that is gaining popularity. One possible downside is that when its cell structure loses water, the fibers can contract and create cracks. Therefore, it may not be suitable flooring in dry climates. You can also find cabinets, countertops, blinds, and other products made from bamboo; it's becoming the darling of sustainable wood products.

As important as floors are, kitchens are one of the most popular remodeling projects, and picking out colors and products consumes more time than does any other part of a project. It can be frustrating as well, because so many cool green products are coming on the market. Every trip to Home

More about sustainable wood floors:

www.woodfloors.org/consumer/

www.laminatefloorings.net/

www.thelaminateflooringsite.com/

www.buildinggreen.com/auth/article.cfm?fileName=061005c.xml

www.corkfloor.com/benefits.html

Depot or Lowes seems to reveal more must-have choices. The next section looks at these green kitchen-remodeling options.

REMODELING YOUR KITCHEN USING GREEN APPLIANCES AND MATERIALS

It's understandable that homeowners take their kitchens so seriously; kitchens are where everyone wants to be—the social center of the home. In addition, it's a major selling point when the home goes on the market. Those homes that don't have updated kitchens tend to languish on the market, and when they finally sell, it's usually at a big discount.

Kitchen remodeling is where triaging your wants and needs is diced most finely. Appliances, of course, should top the list.

Picking Out New Green Appliances

When buying an appliance, remember that it has two price tags: what the appliance costs and what you pay for the energy and water it uses. The more energy efficient an appliance is, the less it's going to cost over time. The first step in selecting kitchen appliances is considering their energy efficiency. Don't be dazzled by styling, color, the dozens of settings you'll never use, or the TV mounted in the door. Look for an Energy Star sticker (www.energystar.gov) that details how energy efficient that product is.

Appliances built prior to 1993 are good candidates for replacement, because newer Energy Star appliances use half as much energy as the older models. In addition, it's common to find new models that substantially exceed minimum Energy Star ratings. It pays to shop different manufacturers, compare models, and read the estimated energy usage stickers. A little math can reveal that the cheaper appliance is not always the best deal.

Here are some appliance replacement tips to keep in mind when shopping for refrigerators, range/ovens, and dishwashers:

- Don't buy a bigger refrigerator than you need; it'll waste energy. Also, don't keep your old fridge for food storage—that will also waste energy; if you need more cold storage, upsize your new fridge.

- Refrigerators with freezer compartments on the side are less efficient than models with freezers above or below the fresh food section.

- Avoid locating the refrigerator next to the range/oven; this will reduce the fridge's efficiency. Enclosing it in a cabinet can also cut down on its efficiency. The coils and compressor need air flow to dissipate heat and operate efficiently. You may need to add a small vent next to the compressor if you tightly enclose the unit on three sides.

- Look for a low water use dishwasher with a booster heater that allows you to set your main water heater at a lower temperature.

- If upgrading your range hood, vent it to the outside. Unvented hoods don't remove VOCs produced during cooking. In addition, gas stoves emit carbon monoxide that you don't want to remain in a tight house.

There are several different types of cook-tops available, from gas to heating elements that create a magnetic field that heats the pan while the top stays cool. These various ranges all have pluses and minuses; it usually boils down to personal choice rather than which product is the most energy efficient. When shopping, look for Energy Star-rated range/ovens.

After appliances, cabinets are often next on the list of kitchen renovations that capture remodelers' enthusiasm. Using sustainable materials is the key to environmentally friendly cabinets.

Upgrading Your Kitchen Cabinets

If you can keep your existing cabinets, you'll not only save money but save resources. Here are some cabinet recycling strategies:

- Often, sanding and staining will make worn cabinets look new.

- If the wood is dark or in bad condition, you can sand and paint cabinets a glossy white.

- Replace the hinges, knobs, and pulls.

- Keep the cabinet frames and replace only the doors and hardware.

- Have a professional reface the cabinets with a wood or laminate veneer.

Sometimes remodeling the kitchen changes the cabinet configuration, and the old ones no longer work. In this case, re-install the cabinets and counters in the basement or garage for a second life.

When one home remodeler couldn't find a use for his old cabinets and counters, he hauled them to his front yard, scrawled a "free, you haul away" sign, and taped it to a cabinet. Less than an hour later, everything was gone.

When you shop for new cabinets, look for Forest Stewardship Council (FSC—www.fscoax.org) certification that the wood is from sustainable sources. Also, the KCMA Certified Cabinet™ seal tells you the cabinets have been tested by the Kitchen Manufacturers Association and meet their standards for durability.

Replacing Your Countertops

Visit a home show or thumb through a home improvement magazine and you'll find dozens of countertop ideas. Some are new laminate colors and patterns, while others make creative use of recycled materials. Options for replacing your countertops have never been so good, especially if you want to make a dramatic showpiece from recycled materials.

You can create impressive results and cut costs by mixing and matching counters and kitchen island surfaces. If you have an island, make it the kitchen's focal point with the higher-priced surface and cut costs on the counters.

One homeowner who needed to cut costs found a stunning piece of granite in the yard of a supplier. Because it was an odd size and one of a kind, the shopper got it for a big discount and installed it on her kitchen island. For her counters, she cut costs by installing laminate with oak edging. The result was an impressive kitchen done on a budget.

Old and new countertop options you may want to consider are:

- Laminate is still the king of countertops. It's economical (up to 60 percent less than other materials) and comes in a wide selection of patterns, colors, and textures. One pattern group mimics granite so closely that you don't know it's not the real thing until you put your hand on it. Laminate manufacturers are more eco-friendly than in the past. Much of their product now comes from recycled materials and uses low VOC, water-based adhesives. Companies such as DuPont, Cambria, Silestone, Formica, Nevamar, and Wilsonart have obtained independent, third-party Greenguard Indoor Air Quality certification that their products comply with strict standards for limited chemical emissions and VOCs.

• Granite has become so popular that designers and homeowners are looking around for other countertop material that has not become so "pedestrian." Although granite is a great countertop choice, both quarrying and the transportation impact on the environment when shipped long distances eliminate much of its eco-friendliness. Look for nearby sources.

• There are many attractive reclaimed and recycled wood countertops on the market. Bamboo, for instance, is becoming popular because it's sustainable and creates a harder-than-maple surface. Another product closely related to wood is recycled paper. When saturated with glue, heated, and compressed, recycled paper creates a stone-like product that makes an attractive and durable counter. When shopping for recycled wood or paper counters, look for those that incorporate low VOC glues and water-based finishes.

• Engineered quartz is made from 95 percent natural stone with 5 percent polymer resins. It's a super-hard, low maintenance surface with the look and feel of natural stone. Available in a variety of color options, it's a good choice. Installed, costs run from $70 to $120 a square foot.

• Recycled solid glass makes an interesting and attractive counter material. It's available in nearly any shape, texture, and color. Cost is typically on the high side, ranging from $60 to $300. However, solid glass makes a great island counter top.

• Take recycled glass fragments, mix them with epoxy resin or cement, and shape the mix into a sheet and you end up with a stunning countertop that your friends with granite will envy. With limitless color configurations, you can easily create a one-of-a-kind counter. This material is on the pricey side, though, at $40 to $90 a square foot. For more information, check out www.icestone.biz and www.enviroglasproducts.com.

• Concrete is an interesting counter material that is growing in popularity. Because these counters are crafted by hand, no two are exactly alike. You get a unique and attractive countertop. Durable and available in many colors and designs, it's a good green choice. You can buy do-it-yourself counter kits from www.buddyrhodes or www.chengdesign.com.

• Mix aluminum shavings with a polymeric resin over a plywood substrate and you get an exciting, distinctive countertop. The shavings can also be anodized to resemble copper or bronze. These counters are on the pricey side at $70 to $150 a square foot. Two sources are www.renewedmaterials.com and www.eleekinc.com.

• Ceramic tile is an oldie but still great counter material. Tiles are especially eco-friendly when made from local clay and set with cement grout rather than high VOC adhesives. Look for natural glazed tiles that are non-porous. Color, size, and texture options are limitless with tile, and they're easy to install. Many home centers teach free tiling classes and rent tile cutters. For an attractive countertop on a budget, tile is hard to beat, especially when you install it yourself. Costs can easily run less than $5 a square foot.

As the market for recycled or green counter material grows, products that are even more exotic will appear on the market. The chances of visiting a model home or friend's house and seeing a counter like yours will become almost zero.

 Green kitchen counter sites:

www.thekitchendesigner.org/journal/2007/10/15/green-kitchen-countertops.html

www.upstatehouse.com/archive/article.php?issue=39&dept=74

www.healthyhomeplans.com/articles/information12.php

www.greenhomeguide.com/index.php/knowhow/entry/641/C219

www.concretenetwork.com

After kitchens, many remodelers tackle bathrooms, where the potential for water and energy savings are fertile ground.

UPGRADING YOUR BATHROOM WITH ECO-FRIENDLY FIXTURES AND MATERIALS

If your bathroom fixtures are more than ten years old, you'll likely gain significant savings by replacing them. For example, manufacturers are bringing out *high-efficiency toilets (HET)* with better tank and bowl hydraulics. These products typically reduce flush volume at least 20 percent below the 1.6-gallon standard. Another tool for water conservation is the EPA's Water Sense program (www.epa.gov/water sense). Similar to the successful Energy Star guide for energy conservation, this program provides a benchmark to use when comparing various fixtures.

When you go shopping for toilets, faucets, and other water-use fixtures, look for a Water Sense label. Products with this label are certified to use at least 20 percent less water and perform as well or better than conventional products. This makes shopping for water-efficient fixtures more certain and less of a crapshoot.

Replacing Toilets, Showers, and Sinks to Conserve Water

Most homes now have three or more toilets that consume 25 to 33 percent of your home's water. If you replace older units with Water Sense-approved fixtures, you'll save at least 20 percent, and that represents big water and money savings.

Some manufacturers are introducing toilets that use 1.28 gallons per flush, which means saving about 10,000 gallons per year. The key to finding these products is the labels.

Showers are another big water user, averaging 17 percent of a household's usage. If you have older showerheads, you'll probably want to replace them with Water Sense-certified models.

Faucets account for another 15 percent of indoor household water use—more than one trillion gallons of water across the United States each year. Even though federal law requires that new faucets not exceed 2.2 gallons per minute (gpm), older faucets can flow at rates as high as 3 to 7 gpm.

High-efficiency bathroom sink faucets and accessories like faucet aerators can reduce this standard flow by more than 30 percent without sacrificing performance. Again, look for the Water Sense label when shopping for replacements.

Shopping for Bathroom Flooring

If you have vinyl bathroom floors, they gotta go. Although vinyl is economical, attractive, and long-lasting, it's toxic and made from polyvinyl chloride (PVC), which is already banned in Europe. With today's airtight houses, you want to keep PVCs to a minimum.

Good flooring choices for bathrooms include the following:

- Tile is the number-one choice for moisture-prone bathrooms. It's durable, waterproof, economical, and available in countless styles and colors.

- Linoleum is a good eco-friendly choice if you don't want to install tile. Its many colors and patterns will compliment any bathroom décor. Use water-based adhesives to keep VOCs to minimum.

- Laminate flooring is a possibility as well, but not recommended. Although some homeowners like laminate floors in the bathroom, these products have a base that's composed of woodchips and glue. If a toilet, shower, or basin overflows, your flooring is likely to swell and buckle.

Changing Your Bathroom Cabinets

Choose wood bathroom cabinets the same way you would for the kitchen. Look for Forest Stewardship Council (FSG) certification that the wood is from renewable sources. Cabinets with wood veneers over particleboard or MDF (medium density fiberboard) need to be sealed unless the glues and stains used are water-based or environmentally safe. Laminate cabinets can be a good choice as well if the adhesives are eco-friendly.

It's also a good idea to seal or paint the inside of your bathroom cabinets. Bathrooms generate humidity big-time, and moist air condenses under the sink when it contacts cold plumbing. A dark and moist environment is mold's dream home.

Keep bathroom cabinets mold-free with frequent inspections; check for leaking plumbing and condensation on the pipes that drips onto the cabinet deck. If metal U traps drip water, you may want to insulate the pipes to prevent this.

Replacing Your Bathroom Lights

Good lighting is important in any bathroom. When shopping for new light bars, look for fixtures that allow enough Energy Star-rated lights to give the fussiest family member enough light. A row of lights over the mirror makes the bath more attractive and enjoyable.

APPENDIX A:
TIPS ON SELLING AN
ECO-FRIENDLY HOME

A frequent criticism about marketing green homes is that buyers are unwilling to pay extra for energy-saving options. However, according to the National Homebuilders Association (NHB), buyers will often spend around $10,000 for energy-saving upgrades for new homes.

It's really a matter of effective marketing. You have some potent tools at hand. Show buyers that by spending a little more up front they can save money over time, emphasize that utility rates are increasing, and point out the opportunity to live a more healthy and independent lifestyle.

But first, you need to find out what your home will sell for in the current market.

DETERMINE A REALISTIC AND COMPETITIVE PRICE

The down and dirty of it is that a home is worth no more and no less than what someone is willing to pay. To get an idea of what someone might be willing to pay for a home in a current market, Realtors and appraisers look at what homes comparable to the one they're pricing have sold for in the last thirty to sixty days. In other words, your neighbors will help determine what your home is worth.

In appraising a home, appraisers use five common points of comparison:

- Square footage. Appraisers typically allow plus or minus 200 square feet in their comparisons.

- Age, an important consideration. Plus or minus five years is commonly used.

- Style. Comparing similar styles is important. You can't equate ranches and Capes, for example.

- Location. Just about anything will sell if it's in a good enough location. Likewise, a great home in a bad location will have problems selling.

- Condition. If problems are not addressed before a home goes on the market, the home may sell for thousands of dollars less than it should.

Appraisers like to identify at least three similar homes for comparison. Since green homes have features that conventional homes don't, appraisers may have a hard time finding close comparables. In that case, they'll most likely add in the cost of the green upgrades minus depreciation. For example, if you spent $23,000 to install a solar power generating system three years ago, its value has likely depreciated. An appraiser would have to research the typical lifespan of your system and calculate how much value is left. He or she would also have to factor in what green upgrades would be worth in your area and current market.

It's important to keep in mind that an appraisal approximates value. It doesn't take into full account the marketability of the home. The house's colors, the way it sits on the lot, interior décor, smell, emotional appeal, and other factors all help determine the final sales price.

For instance, a home appraises for $400,000, but the owners painted the interior bright red, never changed the kitty litter box, and had old green furniture. The home languishes on the market for months; the owners grow desperate and grab a low $325,000 offer. What was the home really worth? It's a moot point. The value is the accepted offer. The market has spoken.

On the flip side, another home appraises for $400,000; it's in a desirable neighborhood with good schools, the décor is coordinated and attractive, and it has super curb appeal. It's likely that several buyers will make offers, and the final sales price could easily rise $10,000, $20,000, or more over appraisal. Here again, the market has spoken.

In short, to determine a sales price for your home, follow these suggestions:

- Look for similar homes that have sold in your area the last few months.

- Ask a Realtor to check the multiple listing (MLS) for comparables that have sold and are for sale.

- Look at similar homes that are now on the market. They will be your competition, and you can price your home slightly lower.

- Don't attempt to price your home based on what you need to make on the sale. Go with market data. After looking at a few homes, buyers quickly become savvy about market values.

- If you or a Realtor can't find recent comparable home sales, hire a professional appraiser. Make sure the appraiser is state certified so that most mortgage lenders will accept the appraisal. It's also a good sales tool, because if anyone questions your price, you have a professional appraisal to back up it up. In addition, when you find a buyer, you can give them the appraisal (actually, they should reimburse you for the cost) and save them a step in the sales process.

MAKE YOUR HOME ATTRACTIVE TO COMPETE WITH OTHERS ON THE MARKET

It's also important in marketing your home to make it as attractive as possible. You'll be competing with other homes on the market, and buyers will be comparing your home closely with others in the price range. Keep in mind that buyers buy first based on emotion; then they justify their decision with numbers, so dirty carpets and peeling paint can hurt you.

Ten things you can do to make your home more attractive, and consequently more competitive, are:

- Declutter, declutter, and declutter some more. Remove family pictures, trophies, excess furniture, and anything else that might distract a potential buyer. It's important for them to visualize their pictures on the walls and how their furniture will look in each room.

- Rent a storage shed and store as much stuff as you can. The less furniture you have in the home, the bigger it looks.

- Repair holes and dings in the walls and paint the rooms a light, neutral color.

- Clean carpets or replace them, as well as other floor coverings that might be a bit threadbare or shabby.

- Be sure that the kitchen is in top condition, because it's extremely important to buyers. See my book *Home Makeovers That Sell: Quick and Easy Ways to Get the Highest Possible Price* (AMACOM, 2007) for detailed information on how to increase your kitchen's charm.

- Ensure that your entryway and your home's curb appeal are enticing, which will encourage buyers to look further. First impressions can make or break a sale.

- If it's winter, have photos available showing your home looking its summertime best.

- Make it easy for a buyer to buy by getting a professional home inspection and using it as a checklist to fix or repair any problems that are found. Use the repair list as a sales tool to show that you've replaced or repaired any problems.

- Because it's likely a buyer will want to take advantage of an Energy Efficient Mortgage (EEM), get a Home Energy Ratings Systems (HERS) report so that he or she knows up-front what energy credits your home will qualify for. See chapter 1 for more info on HERS reports.

- Put together a flyer listing the energy-saving features of your home, along with copies of utility bills documenting the savings a buyer will enjoy.

FINDING BUYERS WHO WANT A GREEN HOME

Marketing your green home also involves fishing where the fish are. In other words, you want to market your home where you're likely to lure green buyers. It's much easier to find a buyer who appreciates what you've done to make your home energy efficient and eco-friendly than to try and convert buyers who aren't of a like mind.

If you're listing your home with a Realtor, most multiple listing services (MLSs) across the country don't detail energy efficient features in their listing check boxes. You'll have to make good use of the remarks section to convey details about your upgrades. In addition, a flyer listing your home's green features and their benefits can be helpful. If it takes two or three pages of text and pictures to cover the features, no problem. Be sure to save a copy of your flyer in PDF format to e-mail to interested buyers.

Some tricks to finding green homebuyers include the following:

- Mail or drop off flyers to architects and suppliers who work with green homes or sell eco-friendly products. For example, the supplier who sold you a solar power system would likely allow you to leave a stack of flyers on the counter. After all, the new owner will need maintenance on the system.

- Go on green home tours and pass out your sale flyers.

- Advertise in local newspapers and magazines that target environmentally aware readers.

- If there are other green homes for sale in your area, organize a green home tour or open houses on a specific weekend. Put together a brochure that lists the homes on the tour and provides a map and details about each home.

- Compile a list of green homeowners in your area and send them a flyer. People tend to associate with those who share their interests, and friends of a green homeowner may be in the market for a home.

- If you can get lists of garden clubs and other green organizations, mail or e-mail them flyers.

- Put your flyer on all the Web sites you can and create a Web site of your own so a buyer can get detailed data. Of course, this Web site address will be on all ads, and your e-mails will have links to it.

HANDLE AN OFFER CAREFULLY

Finally, the moment comes you've been desperately waiting for—you get an offer. An offer is a properly filled out and signed real estate sales agreement with addendums and an earnest money check attached. Anything less than this is what powers the big, colorful balloons you see at fairs.

Why is this so important? Because every state requires that a valid and enforceable real estate contract be in writing, signed by both parties, and have valuable consideration. Normally the consideration is a personal or cashier's check, but it can be a promissory note or anything of value that both parties agree to.

Addendums attached to the offer can be for FHA/VA financing, additional terms, inspections, lead-based paint disclosures, or other federal- or state-mandated forms.

It's likely that an offer will come in low, because buyers want to get the best deal they can and believe that a good way to start out is to underbid. Your best response is not to take the offer as a personal insult and get upset. Instead, sharpen your pencil and work the math. What's the lowest price you're willing to accept? Figure that out, write up a counter-offer, and send it back to the buyer or buyers' agent.

Another timesaving approach is to ask your agent to call the buyers' agent with your counter and bounce it back and forth verbally until everyone comes to an agreement. Then put it in writing and have everyone sign it.

Once you're ready to accept an offer, here are some tips, as well as some traps, to look out for:

- Make sure a pre-approval letter accompanies an offer.

- Call the lender (or have your agent call) and verify that the buyer is really pre-approved. Ask specifically if their credit and income will support the loan. Many times lenders give out these letters before they've verified the buyers' application data.

- Have on hand a half dozen addendum forms for counter-offers and changes.

- Understand all the subject-tos and conditions in the offer. For instance, most states have deadlines for inspections, appraisals, loan approvals, and closing dates that are in the offer. The buyer may want to write additional conditions in an addendum as well. It's helpful to make a simple table that lists the offer's conditions and their deadlines so you can stay on top of them.

- Once a condition to the offer, such as an inspection or appraisal, is completed, remove it with an addendum signed by all parties. Number addendums 1/x, 2/x, and so on; the mortgage lender and title company require this so they can account for them as the transaction moves along toward closing.

- Home inspections and appraisals are two speed bumps that occur in most offers. Typically, a week or so after you sign an offer, the home inspection comes back recommending a few repairs or conditions. If the buyers feel all or some of the repairs are important to their buying the home, they'll write an addendum requesting you take care of them. Your options are to fix the problems, refuse, or open negotiations on what you will or will not do. This is why it's better to get an inspection before you put the home one the market—you won't get blindsided a week or two before closing.

- Another item you want to get up-front is payoffs on all mortgages you have on the house. Sometimes there's a pre-payment penalty if you pay off a mortgage early that can impact your selling the home.

For a more complete coverage on home selling strategies, see my book *A Survival Guide for Selling a Home* (AMACOM, 2005).

One of the biggest keys to a smooth sale is to line up your ducks before you put the home on the market.

APPENDIX B:

GREEN HOME TAX BREAKS AND

FINANCIAL INCENTIVES

Federal, state, and city governments as well as utility companies are lining up to help you build or remodel your home to be more environmentally responsible and energy efficient. These financial incentives can dramatically shorten the break-even point of install costs versus monthly savings.

TAX CREDITS

A tax credit—local, state, or federal—is generally more valuable than an equivalent tax deduction because it reduces tax dollar-for-dollar, while a deduction only removes a percentage of the tax owed. Beginning in tax year 2006, you can itemize qualifying energy-saving purchases on your federal income tax form, as discussed next, which will lower the total amount of tax owed.

Federal Tax Incentives

As of this writing in early 2008, most of the residential tax credits (windows, doors, roofs, insulation, HVAC, and non-solar water heaters) expired. However, tax credits for solar water heaters and solar panels were extended. It's expected that in 2008 an extension of previous tax credits will be passed.

You can claim one federal credit for up to $4,000 to cover 30 percent of a photovoltaic system's cost and another 30 percent credit for up to $2,000 for a thermal system. These are credits, not deductions, so they reduce your tax bill dollar for dollar. More tax credit information is available at the following Web sites:

- www.irs.gov/pub/irs-drop/n-06-26.pd
- http://aceee.org/energy/state/index.htm
- www.greenenergyohio.org/page.cfm?pageID=710
- www.dsireusa.org/summarytables/FinEE.cfm?&CurrentPageID=7&EE=1&RE=1
- www.energytaxincentives.org/consumers/solar.php

State and Local Tax Incentives

Many states give tax credits in addition to the federal ones. For example, New York allows you to claim a tax credit equal to 25 percent of the cost of solar heating or power systems, up to $5,000. It also exempts solar systems from sales tax and gives homeowners a 15-year property tax exemption on the system. You can find out what incentives your state and city offers by checking out these two Web sites:

- www.ases.org
- www.dsireusa.org/index.cfm?EE=1&RE=1

Local Rebates from Utilities

Local utilities also give rebates for upgrading energy-saving products. In addition, your utility bills contain information on offered programs, like hauling away your old appliances for free when you upgrade to new Energy Star products.

As energy efficiency gains more support, you can expect government agencies and utilities to develop new or implement or increase existing their incentives. Scan your utility bills each month for new programs, watch for news releases, and check the previous Web sites for incentive changes. To find out what's available in your area go to www.energystar.gov/index.cfm?fuseaction=rebate.rebate_locator and type in your zip code.

APPENDIX C:
THE TEN BIGGEST MISTAKES
GREEN HOME REMODELERS MAKE

MISTAKE 1: Tackling the fun interior upgrades first—such as kitchens, counters, and appliances—and then running out of money

Upgrading the home's envelope (house wrap and roof) to be watertight and insulated should be your first priority; energy-saving upgrades such as windows, furnace, and solar water heaters should follow.

Before you start, make a list of the projects you want to accomplish. Next, prioritize the projects based on importance and the practical perspective suggested above.

Sometimes it's tough to fight the temptation to replace ugly kitchen countertops or battered appliances up-front, but doing the critical upgrades first can save big bucks when winter winds blow and the rains descend.

MISTAKE 2: Upgrading a home before making sure the neighborhood will support the green upgrades and improvements

When shopping for a home to upgrade, look carefully at the area first. You may feel you'll live in the house forever, but job and life changes make Americans a mobile society. The national average of how long homeowners stay in a home is between six and seven years.

If you have a 2,600 square foot home and need 3,600 square feet, it may be better to sell and buy in a neighborhood of similar-size homes before adding on to your home. In some cases, homebuyers who remodel their homes find they can't sell because they've over-improved for the area. Few buyers are likely to pay an extra $20,000 to $40,000 above neighborhood market values, even for an energy efficient house.

Before planning your remodeling project, have a Realtor print out a list of how much homes have sold for in your area. Note what the remodeled homes have sold for compared with the ones that haven't been updated. That will give you an idea of expected return on investment in case you want to sell.

MISTAKE 3: Neglecting to take proactive steps to prevent mold and wood rot in the basement

Installing a vapor barrier on inside basement walls allows water vapor to condense between the wall and plastic barrier. It's better to install a layer of extruded polystyrene foam (XPS) insulation on the inside wall, then furring strips or framing followed by drywall.

Waterproofing coatings you can apply to concrete and cinderblock walls also help stop water from infiltrating. However, if the problem is condensation, you may have to install a humidifier or ductwork from the furnace to heat the space.

In the case that water comes from a high water table or seasonal water infiltration, you may want to invest in a sump pump. This is a small pump installed in the bottom of a small well in the basement floor. When water enters the well, the pump kicks in and pumps water into a drain.

If you have this type of water problem, consult with a plumbing contractor to see how big a unit you need and where it should be installed.

MISTAKE 4: Allowing moisture into crawlspaces that causes wood rot and mold

Many homes have vents that allow warmer humid air to enter cooler crawlspaces, where it condenses, rotting wood and encouraging mold.
Treat the space like a full basement; heat it in the winter and cool it in the summer by installing an air supply duct. Also, install a vapor barrier over the floor and insulate the walls. This should keep the space at a constant temperature and control humidity. Like keeping basements dry, it's just as

important to keep crawlspaces dry to prevent having to do costly repairs later on.

MISTAKE 5: Using the space between studs or joists for heating or cooling ductwork

When you shortcut and try to save money by using the space between studs or joists for heating or cooling ductwork, you're asking for trouble. Humid, contaminated air sucked into these spaces can create a mold-friendly environment. Using these spaces also allows contaminated air from garages that may contain carbon monoxide to enter living spaces.

If mold from humid air gets into these spaces, demo costs to get to the problem and clean it up can add up to big bucks.

Recently, a home in Utah had black mold that spread so far through the walls and floors that it had to be torn down to the foundation.

MISTAKE 6: Neglecting to vent an air- and watertight house

New and energy efficient remodeled homes have air and water proof housewraps that are installed before the siding goes on. Essentially, you're living in a plastic bag, and if you don't vent the home, it's likely to result in a buildup of indoor pollution. New and remodeled energy efficient homes need air intake and exhaust vents with heat exchanges to prevent indoor air pollution and energy loss.

Equally importantly, bathrooms, laundry rooms, and range hoods should have their own separate fans that vent to the outside. Avoid venting to the garage, attic, basement, or crawlspace, which in many areas is a violation of building codes.

MISTAKE 7: Failing to ensure that gutters and downspouts are in good condition and that water is routed away from the house's foundation

Water seeping into a crawlspace or basement is an invitation for mold and rot to move in; and they are tenants you don't want. It pays to make sure that your gutters and downspouts are in good working order and aren't channeling water into a window well or close to the foundation. It's also important to correct any landscaping that doesn't route water away from your home's foundation. You may want to walk around the home in a heavy rain storm (with umbrella, of course) and see how well your gutter system is handling the water flow. While you're outside in the rain, check runoff from your landscaping to make sure it's flowing away from the house.

MISTAKE 8: Using space heaters, gas fireplaces, and candles without proper ventilation

Any appliance that burns with a flame adds carbon monoxide and other pollutants to your indoor air. Gas and kerosene space heaters and unvented fireplaces are especially bad sources of indoor air pollution. Even if you open a window, you won't get rid of the pollution.

An alternative to burning scented candles is to use a small electric appliance that heats the wax and releases the scent without a flame. Yes, it's unromantic, but then allergies and asthma are more unromantic—and expensive.

MISTAKE 9: Neglecting to follow through on verifying licensing, insurance coverage, and checking to see whether there are any unresolved complaints when hiring a contractor

All too often, news reports carry stories of homeowners getting scammed by people posing as contractors and unscrupulous tradespeople. This happens because people don't take a few easy precautions, such as:

- Asking for referrals that you can contact to check out previous work before you commit

- Avoiding "good deals," when contractors knock on your door saying they have a job nearby and will give you a super deal. Good contractors never go door-to-door looking for business; they are so busy that often you practically have to beg them to consider your project.

- Asking to see copies of contractors' licenses and insurance coverage policies

- And most importantly, never paying for the job up front. At most you should pay 25 percent to get started, with the balance due on completion of small jobs. If you're told contractors don't have the credit to get materials for the job and that they need the whole amount up-front, it's likely a scam.

MISTAKE 10: Failing to look to the house as a holistic system

If you change one component, it affects all the others. For example, if you incorporate passive solar heat and upgrade insulation, you can downsize furnace and air conditioner sizes.

Likewise, wrapping, insulating, and sealing air leaks will change the way air is replaced in the home. Often a ventilation system is needed, and you may have to install a new heating system and AC to accommodate ductwork that vents the whole house. Because of the interconnectedness of green building techniques, it's often advisable to use a professional to help you develop a holistic plan.

APPENDIX D:
ECO-FRIENDLY RESOURCES

ASSOCIATIONS

National Association of Home Builders (NAHB)
www.nahb.org/local_association_search_form.aspx

National Association of the Remodeling Industry (NARI)
www.nari.org/search/chapters

American Society of Heating, Refrigerating and Air-Conditioning Engineers (ASHRAE) www.ashrae.org

Solar Energy Industries Association (SEIA)
www.seia.org

GreenGuard Environmental Institute (GEI) Indoor air quality certification programs www.greenguard.org

AIR/WATER SYSTEMS

Magna Tec
www.scaleaway.com, (877) 854-7638

Pure n' Natural Systems, Inc.
www.purennatural.com, (800) 237-9199

Waterwise
www.waterwise.com, (800) 874-9028

BUILDING ENERGY EFFICIENT HOMES

www.eere.energy.gov/buildings/building_america/

www.asc.org

www.greenhomeguide.com/index.php/product/C237

www.conservationeconomy.net

www.buildinggreen.com/menus

www.greenerchoices.org

www.nahb.org/fileUpload_details.aspx?contentTypeID=7&contentID=1994

FINDING ARCHITECTURAL SERVICES

www.usgbc.org

www.greenhomeguide.com

www.greenbuildingblocks.com

www.moderngreenliving.com

GEOTHERMAL HEATING AND COOLING

www.waterfurnace.com

www.energystar.gov/index.cfm?c=geo_heat.pr_geo_heat_pumps - 16k -

www.geoexchange.org

www.geothermal.marin.org/pwrheat.html - 38k

GREEN FLOORING

www.themarmoleumstore.com, (866) 627-6653

www.greenhomeguide.com/index.php/knowhow/topic/C220 - 26k

www.enn.com/green_building/article/29222

GREEN LANDSCAPING INFORMATION

www.epa.gov/greenacres

www.jetsongreen.com/2007/03/green_building_.html

www.greenlivingideas.com/landscaping/index.php

INSULATION INFORMATION

www.nuwood.com, (800) 748-0128

www.ornl.gov/sci/roofs+walls/insulation/ins_01.html

INTERESTING GREEN WEB SITES

www.energystar.gov/index.cfm?fuseaction=home_energy_advisor.showGetInput
*Web site where you can key in your zip code and get suggestions for
upgrades in your area*

www.greenfestivals.org/content/view/767/390/
*A list of green festivals that bring together builders, suppliers, and
innovators in green tech*

www.buildinggreen.com/press/topten2007/index.cfm

RENEWABLE ENERGY

http://www.dsireusa.org/

ROOFING

www.conservationtechnology.com

www.owenscorning.com/around/roofing

www.roofing.com

www.roofhelp.com

www.metalroofing.com/

www.energystar.gov/index.cfm?c=roof_prods.pr_roof_products - 12k

SOLAR ENERGY INFORMATION

www.ases.org

www.findsolar.com

www.irecusa.org

www.nrel.gov

www.rredc.nrel.gov/solar/codes_algs/PVWATTS/

www.solar-rating.org

TAX INCENTIVES

www.dsireusa.org
State-by-state listing of incentives

www.energystar.gov/index.cfm?c=products.pr_tax_credits

WINDOWS

www.nfrc.org

www.efficientwindows.org

www.eere.energy.gov/consumer

RECOMMENDED BOOKS AND MANUALS

The Green Gardener, Working with Nature, Not Against It
Brenda Little
(Silverleaf Press, 2007)

1001 Ways to Save the Earth
Joanna Yarrow
(Chronicle, 2007)

The Carbon Buster's Home Energy Handbook
Godo Stoyke
(New Society, 2007)

The Lazy Environmentalist
Josh Aorfman
(Stewart, Tabori & Chang, 2007)

Natural Timber Frame Homes
Wayne Bingham, Jerod Pfeffer
(Gibbs Smith, 2007)

Off-the-Grid Homes
Lori Ryker
(Gibbs Smith, 2007)

The Ultimate New-Home Buying Guide
Jeff and Susan Treganowan
(Maple Leaf Press, 2001)

Sun, Wind & Light: Architectural Design Strategies
G.Z. Brown, Mark DeKay
(John Wiley & Sons, Inc., 2000)

The People's Guide to Basic Solar Power
William L. Seavey
(www.powerfromsun.com)

Xeriscape Gardening
Tom Stephens
(MacMillan, 1991)

Xeriscape Handbook
Gayle Weinstein
(Fulcrum Publishing, 1999)

Xeriscape Color Guide
Edited By Davis Winger
(Fulcrum Publishing, 1999)

Green Building Products
The Greenspec® Guide to Residential Building Materials
Alex Wilson, Mark Pirpkotn
(New Society Publishers, 2005)

Green Remodeling
David Johnston, Kim Master
(New Society Publishers, 2004)

PUBLICATIONS

Inspired House
(www.inspiredhouse.com)

Fine Homebuilding Magazine
(www.finehomebuilding.com)

Natural Home
(www.naturalhomemagazine.com)

Mother Earth News
(www.motherearthnews.com)

This Old House
(www.thisoldhouse.com)

Ultimate Home Design
(www.ultimatehomedesign.com)

INDEX

Look for These Informative Real Estate Titles at www.amacombooks.org/go/realestate